Illustrator:
Jose L. Tapia

Editor:
Walter Kelly, M.A.

Editorial Project Manager:
Karen J. Goldfluss, M.S. Ed.

Editor-in-Chief:
Sharon Coan, M.S. Ed.

Art Director:
Elayne Roberts

Associate Designer:
Denise Bauer

Cover Artist:
Elayne Roberts

Product Manager:
Phil Garcia

Imaging:
David Bennett

Publishers:
Rachelle Cracchiolo, M.S. Ed.
Mary Dupuy Smith, M.S. Ed.

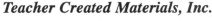

How to Be an Effective Teacher

Authors:

Kelley Dos Santos Kremer, M. Ed. and Steve Reifman, M. Ed.

Teacher Created Materials

Teacher Created Materials, Inc.
P.O. Box 1040
Huntington Beach, CA 92647
ISBN-1-55734-469-8

©1996 Teacher Created Materials, Inc.   Made in U.S.A.

Table of Contents

Introduction

Teachers need a great deal of information in order to do their jobs well. Yet we do not usually have the time needed to seek out, read, and organize this information. If we had the luxury of more time, we would be able to read entire texts on parent conferencing, learning centers, and the dozens of other topics about which we need expertise. Since most teachers lack this time, an urgent need exists for a resource book that would present information of this nature in a simple, straightforward manner. It is our sincere hope that this book can serve as a one-stop resource guide for teachers who need, in a very short time, a great deal of information in areas other than the curriculum.

How to Be an Effective Teacher is divided into five sections:

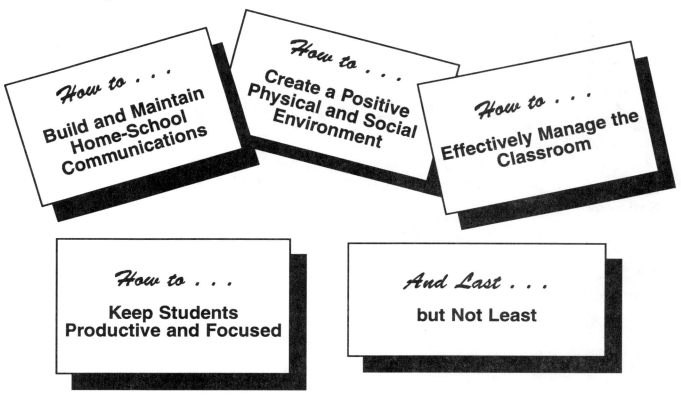

How to . . .
Build and Maintain Home-School Communications

How to . . .
Create a Positive Physical and Social Environment

How to . . .
Effectively Manage the Classroom

How to . . .
Keep Students Productive and Focused

And Last . . .
but Not Least

We have purposely avoided providing information which pertains to subject matter, content, or the curriculum. We leave the provision of that type of knowledge to university training courses, curriculum guides, and the scores of other resource books which focus on this area. Instead, we focus on the daily, "extra-curricular" aspects of organizing and managing a classroom, the ones which every teacher encounters but which all too often do not receive the attention they deserve.

Although much of the information provided in this book has its foundation in educational theory, you will not be impeded with the theorist's terms or jargon. Instead, we have chosen to present the information in an easy-to-read list format. Feel free to pick and choose the suggestions you think will work with your unique group of students at your particular grade level. We have tried very hard to compile and simplify information without trivializing it. Your personal style of teaching will be consistent with some of the suggestions we have provided and be inconsistent with others. In any case, a wide variety of suggestions is included. Choose those ideas which best suit your needs. Good luck!

How to. . . .

Build and Maintain Home-School Communications

Working Together

While we are the official teachers of our students, parents are their children's first and most important teachers. Not all teachers are parents, yet all parents are teachers. If children are to succeed in school, it is vital that parents and teachers work together. Parents need to know how to reinforce what the teacher is doing in school, and teachers need to know what factors at home are affecting their students' performance. Frequent communication is necessary so that all the parties involved have the information they need to perform their roles adequately.

Following are specific suggestions to promote working together.

How to Promote Working Together

✔ Call home before the school year begins to introduce yourself to both your students and their parents.

✔ Send home a letter the first day of school discussing the year ahead. In this letter you may choose to include some biographical information about yourself, your goals for the year, your classroom management system, and your educational philosophy. It is also a good idea to attach a blank page at the end of your letter so that parents can let you know about any concerns, abilities, or interests they or their children may have. They then sign and return this sheet to you. A sample letter is provided on page 8. You may wish to adapt its contents and length to meet your needs.

✔ Draw up a home-school contract outlining the class rules, expectations, and guidelines for the parents and students to sign. Taking this step gives a sense of ownership to families over what occurs in the classroom.

✔ Maintain an interactive home-school communications journal for each student. This journal should be transported back and forth by the student. It allows the teacher to communicate regularly with parents on an informal basis. A sample journal entry is provided on page 10.

✔ Assemble a list of community organizations whose addresses and phone numbers parents may need. (A list of community resources is provided on page 15.)

Working Together *(cont.)*

How to Promote Working Together *(cont.)*

✔ Send home a weekly class newsletter. You can use this newsletter to summarize the previous week, offer a sneak preview of the week ahead, describe various features of your classroom, highlight pieces of student work, promote upcoming events, and ask for special favors. A sample newsletter is provided on page 11.

✔ If possible, make written communication available in any necessary language.

✔ Organize workshops and arrange for guest speakers on matters of interest to parents.

✔ Have a potluck meal in your classroom. You may want to schedule it to coincide with one of the workshops mentioned above.

✔ Invite parents to participate in special class events such as holiday parties, cooking activities, or art projects.

✔ Incorporate the expertise that parents possess into your curriculum. If you are doing a unit on the legal system, invite a few parents who are lawyers, clerks, or judges to share their knowledge and experience. The type of work a parent does is not important. What is important is the fact that you include them.

✔ Consider making a home visit. Parents are often more comfortable relating to teachers on their "home turf" where the atmosphere is more informal.

✔ Call or send notes home frequently to share good news as well as bad. Parents are accustomed to hearing from teachers only when the news is bad. Surprise them. Sending postcards through the mail is one creative way to relay this type of information.

✔ Survey students and parents periodically about various features of your classroom. This shows them that their opinions matter to you and that you value their input.

✔ Actively solicit parents to volunteer in the classroom. Their labor helps out tremendously while their mere presence shows the students that they care about the education of young people.

Working Together *(cont.)*

How to Promote Working Together *(cont.)*

✔ Put a suggestion box in the classroom. Invite both students and parents to contribute their ideas.

✔ Record a daily homework hotline so that parents can call to find out the day's assignments. Students often claim to have no homework, but their parents suspect otherwise. The homework hotline allows parents to check for sure. It is also a great way for absent students to find out about their assignments.

✔ Distribute a homework sheet for parents to sign in order to show that they have monitored their child's efforts. Many teachers attach a sheet of this kind to a "homework packet" which contains all the assignments for a given week. Two sample homework packet cover sheets can be found on page 13.

✔ Have your students write invitations to their families for major class events. Invitations written by students are much more personal, and usually cuter, than ones done by the teacher.

✔ Maintain a reasonable open door policy in your classroom. Parents should feel comfortable approaching teachers, but they also need to know that it must be done during non-school hours.

✔ Try to become involved in neighborhood and community events. Participating in community clean ups, canned food drives, and recycling rallies sends the message that you view the school as not just the place where you work, but as part of a larger community that you care deeply about.

✔ Encourage parents to observe in your class. Parents are more likely to want to volunteer and are more likely to empathize with you once they have seen what actually goes on in your class.

✔ Distribute a calendar of major school and class events. Doing so gives parents the advance notice they need so that they can organize their schedules around these events. Have students take part in filling these out. See page 16 for a blank calendar.

✔ Establish a phone tree. A phone tree serves as an effective way to communicate important messages to all parents quickly.

✔ Send home occasional tips which will help parents help their children at home. Parents want very much to assist their children in their educational pursuits, but they are often unsure how to do it. Tips about how to help with homework, just to name one example, can be extremely helpful for them. You can incorporate these tips into the weekly class newsletter. For more information about how you can help parents help their children, see page 14.

Beginning of the Year Sample Letter

Date _____

Dear Parent(s),

This is the letter I promised you last week. In this letter I will discuss my plans for the upcoming year. For those of you who have not yet received any information from me, I would like to take this opportunity to introduce myself. My name is_____, and I will be your child's teacher this year. This is my first year at_____, and I am very eager to begin what I hope will be a rewarding career here.

I am a firm believer in the idea that schools must help the parent raise the child. With this belief in mind, I hope to work very closely with you this year to see that your child gets the most out of our year together as he or she possibly can. I don't have to tell you that a challenging world awaits your child, and I feel that it is our responsibility to work as a team in order to prepare your child to succeed in this world as a productive worker, concerned citizen, trusted family member, good friend, intelligent consumer, and caring adult. I know that this year is just one of many that your child will spend in school, but I strongly feel that the possibilities for intellectual, social, and personal growth are tremendous.

I have high expectations for my students. The work we do will be challenging. I will structure our assignments, though, so that if the students put forth the effort, they will be successful. It is important for the students to learn at a young age that effort leads to success. The students will not have to face these challenges on their own. I will be with them every step of the way, providing assistance whenever they reach the point where they have done as much as they possibly can on their own.

I am committed to creating an upbeat, productive classroom environment. The students will play an active role in their own learning. Not only will much of the learning be hands-on, but also the students will have a large voice in determining what this work actually will be. Every attempt will be made to make the work meaningful to the students.

I want to engage their interest, get them excited about learning, get them to realize the importance of learning, and encourage them to take pride in and ownership over their work. School can be an exciting place, and our class will be such a place once I make it clear to the students that I am counting on their participation and enthusiasm to help shape the form of our classroom.

(*continued on next page*)

Beginning of the Year Sample Letter *(cont.)*

I will begin the year by strongly enforcing our basic classroom rules, which we as a class will create. Students will be rewarded for exemplary behavior. Such rewards will include (but will not be limited to) praise, a positive note or telephone call home, and free time. Conversely, punishment will follow unacceptable behavior. These consequences will include (but, again, will not be limited to) loss of part of recess, loss of opportunity to serve as a classroom monitor, a note or phone call home, and—if it comes to this—a conference with the student so that we can deal effectively with any ongoing problem.

I would like for us to remain in regular communication with each other throughout the year. It would be a shame if parent conferences, Back-to-School Night, and Open House were the only times that we were able to meet. I will be sending home periodic newsletters to alert you to major events, activities, and units that our class will be doing. If there is anything that you do not understand, would like to comment on, or have a question about, please feel free to call me here at school, send a note to school with your child, or visit me here before or after school. If I am not available when you call me at school, I will make every attempt to return your call within 48 hours. In addition, I strongly encourage you to come into our classroom to volunteer. Any amount of time that you can give would be greatly appreciated. Our door is always open. If you feel that you don't have specific skills or abilities to add to our classroom, let me assure you that is not the case. There are always dozens of things with which you can assist us. Furthermore, your very presence in the classroom sends the message to the children that you care about the education of our community's young people. The value of this message cannot be overestimated. I look forward to speaking with you soon.

Please use the space provided to let me know any information about your child that you feel will help me perform my duties as teacher more effectively. In addition, please sign your name on the bottom of this sheet where indicated. Even if you write very little, or even nothing, please sign this sheet, tear it off, and give it to your child to return to me as soon as possible.

- -

Sincerely,

Comments:_____

_____

_____

_____

Signature _____

Date _____

Sample Communications Journal

(Date) _____

Dear (Parents or Guardian),

I just wanted to let you know what a terrific job your daughter did today during our science investigation. She was an active participant during the experiment and also added positively to our class discussion. She should be very proud of herself.

Sincerely,

_____
(Teacher Signature)

(Date) _____

Dear (Teacher),

Thank you for taking the time to inform me about Jessica's progress. My wife and I greatly appreciate it.

_____
(Parent or Guardian Signature)

Sample Newsletter

Volume 1, September 12, 19____

What's Going On in Room 20?

A Weekly Newsletter

Building a Classroom Library

The first major project of the year involves building a classroom library. Each day the children will have an opportunity to read silently for about 15 minutes. During this time they are free to choose from among all the books in our library. So far, the books in our classroom have come from the school library, the public library, and my home. While our class collection has gotten off to a promising start, we could really use your help in adding to it. If you have any extra books, magazines, or newspapers that would be appropriate for first and second graders, we would greatly appreciate your letting us borrow or keep them. Thanks!

Giving the Gift of Reading

The members of Room 20 have a special way of celebrating birthdays. Instead of spending money on cookies or a cake for the children each time one of the students has a birthday, we request that the family instead purchase a book and give it to the class as a special gift. This approach allows the class to have an enduring, tangible commemoration of these special events.

Volunteering

I would again like to invite the parents of Room 20 to volunteer in our classroom. Whatever time you can spare would be greatly appreciated. There are always plenty of things that need to be done, but more important than the work you do is the fact that your presence shows the children you care about what is happening in their classroom. If you are interested in volunteering, please find me after school or leave a message for me in the office. Thanks!

News from Fifth Grade

Special Events

- Friday 11/4 Staff Development
- Friday 11/11 Veterans Day
- Wednesday 11/29 Report Cards
- Thursday 12/1 Parent Conferences begin

Curriculum

✎ Language Arts

We are finishing the novel *The Sign of the Beaver*. We were able to create many wonderful projects from this unit. Each student wrote and illustrated a haiku, which several of them presented at the Honors Assembly. They created birch bark paintings representing their families. From a descriptive paragraph, the students drew wigwams. We discovered how well 5th graders can sew! Thank you to all parent volunteers for helping us make our moccasins look so authentic! The culminating activity for *The Sign of the Beaver* will focus on friendship. Our book project for the month of November is based on an historical fiction novel. Students are to create a letter written by the protagonist to themselves. This will be due on November 30. Our text core literature book is historical fiction, *The Terrible Wave*.

Sample Newsletter *(cont.)*

Volume 1, September 12, 19____

What's Going On in Room 20?

A Weekly Newsletter

Curriculum *(cont.)*

✐ Math

During the month of October we were busy completing our first unit, LARGE numbers. We then jumped right into multiplication. We are very happy to announce how well the students know their multiplication facts. However, multiplying numbers 7 and 8 still causes trouble! We will end our multiplication unit on November 10 and have our unit test on that date. The students have created several books—*Deep in the Forest*, *What Is Multiplication?*, and *The Price Is Right!* Our next unit will be on division, beginning November 10. The Guessing Jar is still a favorite! Thank you Bryce for bringing in three different jars with Halloween treats!

✐ Social Studies

Heritage Day has finally arrived! I hope you get a chance to share in the celebration on Monday, November 7th, in the art room. (Check times on the yellow schedule that went home.) We have completed our maps, reports, flags, family trees, and ancestor dolls with much success and pride in our heritage! A big thanks to those parents who helped in the classroom and for your generous donations of fabric, glue, sequins, etc. You're terrific! Our next unit, "The First People of the Americas," will be fairly short. We will study five Native American cultures and have an exam on Friday, November 18. From there, we "sail" into a unit called "Geography and Exploration."

✐ Science

On Tuesday we started a new unit on models and designs. All the activities in the unit are hands-on; therefore, students will not have many notes to study and review. It is imperative that students be in school to participate in the learning opportunities. Because of the hands-on activities in the unit, part of the assessment will involve manipulatives. Green science folders, the culmination of our scientific process unit, were returned to students on Tuesday. Please ask to see these folders! Students were given the grading rubric and instructions for the folders one week before the date they were due. Please ask your child to explain what a scientific black box is!

Next Science Test—Tuesday, November 15

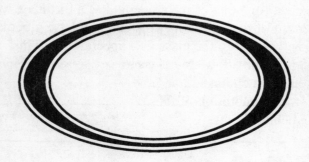

Reminder: The Egg Contraption Project is due the second week of December.

Sample Homework Cover Sheets

Dictation Packet #3	Name_____

Here is this week's homework packet. The following is a schedule of activities for the week.

MON	Copy the dictation passage in the space provided. A copy of the dictation passage can be found on the following page.
TUES	Pick the five words that you think are the hardest in the dictation passage. Write them three times each.
WED	The boy loved the giving tree very much. Write a sentence of your own describing something you love. Then draw a picture which explains your sentence.
THURS	Please read the dictation passage to your child and have him/her write it on the paper provided. Since this is the format I use each Friday, it is good practice for your child.

Parent Signature _____

Homework Packet #30	Name_____

Here is this week's homework packet. The following is a schedule of activities for the week. I am including two bonus words in the spelling list which your child can learn if he or she wishes. These words are not required but are offered for an extra challenge.

MON	Copy each spelling word three times.
TUES	Fill in the blanks so that each word is spelled correctly.
WED	1. Circle the words that are spelled correctly and cross out the incorrect spellings. 2. Solve the math problems.
THURS	Please dictate each word to your child and have him/her write it on the paper provided. Since this is the format I use each Friday, it is good practice for your child.

Parent Signature _____

Helping Parents Help Their Children

A significant aspect of the home-school relationship involves helping parents help their children at home. Parents are usually very eager to play a major role in the education of their children, but they are rarely told how to do so. Unfortunately, teachers often interpret this parental uncertainly as unwillingness or apathy. Feelings of this sort weaken the home-school connection, a bond which should be growing stronger as the school year progresses. The following list contains some suggestions that you should share with the parents of your students. When you provide parents with this type of information, you are equipping them and their children with habits and attitudes that will last them a lifetime.

Ways to Help Children at Home

✔ Commit yourselves to playing an active role in your child's education. Many parents leave the responsibility for their child's education with the teacher. This practice is unwise. Parents must remain involved on a consistent basis.

✔ Repeatedly express to your child that doing well in school and getting an excellent education are essential prerequisites for living a productive, enjoyable life. You can never repeat this message too many times.

✔ Develop a homework policy with your child: No television until all homework is complete? No play time? Discuss questions like these with your child so that both of you are clear about your expectations for home study.

✔ Provide your child with a quiet place to study. If you can afford to buy your child a desk, that would be wonderful. The important point is that your child has a consistent place to study where nobody will disturb him/her. Providing such an atmosphere will not only enable your child to have an easier time studying but also send a clear message that you think doing homework is important.

✔ Monitor your child's progress on homework assignments every night.

✔ Discuss school events and happenings with your child as often as possible.

✔ Request from your child's teacher a reading list of the educational publications that have most deeply influenced him/her, whether they be books, journals, or magazines, so that you can discover which ideas inform his/her practice.

✔ Help keep your child on schedule during long-term projects and while preparing for tests.

✔ Look through your child's papers each day to ensure that all school notices find their way to you.

✔ Do not hesitate to express to the teacher any concerns you may have about your child's education.

✔ Do your best to make sure that your child takes to school all the supplies needed each day.

Community Resources

While it is well-known that teachers often provide assistance to their students about important matters, it is less well-known that there are also times when a teacher can offer such assistance to parents. If a parent has just recently moved into your area or for some other reason is unfamiliar with the resources of your community, it is advisable that teachers have important information ready to share. Maintaining an up-to-date resource list is, therefore, a good idea. Below are the names of some agencies, organizations, and services whose phone numbers might be useful to have on this list.

Community Resources	Telephone Number
Police Department	
Fire Department	
FEMA	
Department of Social Services	
Summer Camps	
After-School Programs	
Child Care Centers	
Parks and Playgrounds	
Little Leagues	
Museums	
Theaters	
Art and Music Schools	
Charities	
Red Cross	
Literacy Groups	
Elected Officials (School Board)	
Pet Adoption Facilities and Animal Shelters	
Hospitals	
Veterans' Groups	
Legal Services	
Head Start/Pre-Schools	
Adult Education Courses	
Salvation Army	
Alcoholics Anonymous	

School and Class Events Calendar for

_____ (month)

Sunday	Monday	Tuesday	Wednesday	Thursday	Friday	Saturday

How to. . .

Create a Positive Physical and Social Environment

Using Physical Space Effectively

The ways in which you employ your wall space greatly affect the type of environment you create in your classroom. It is important to design walls that are aesthetically pleasing, functional, and consistent with your philosophy of education. There is always the tendency to want to cover every bit of open wall space, but try to resist this temptation. More is not necessarily better. In addition, place items in locations that most teachers often overlook, such as on closet doors or above sinks. After all, students spend a great deal of time looking at these usually empty spaces.

"On the Wall" Ideas

✔ Display posters of the classroom rules, rewards, and consequences.

✔ Create a calendar. Use bright colors, patterns, or perhaps a different numbering system. For example, you could try Roman numerals, a periodic table of elements numbering system, or Morse Code. In the primary grades the calendar is a wonderful medium for introducing, extending, and reviewing mathematical concepts. For more information about how to use calendars for this purpose, please consult Mary Baratta-Lorton's *Mathematics Their Way*.

✔ Randomly select a "Student of the Week" to feature on a bulletin board. To boost the self-esteem of the Student of the Week, sit him/her on a special chair and have the other students take turns saying what they like about that student. Record these statements and post them on a bulletin board along with a "Student of the Week" certificate, a picture of that student, and a sample of that student's work. For a variation of this idea, please see the insert which follows the list entitled, "Providing Individual Attention."

✔ Display students' work. Be sure to include everyone's work so that your students do not view the posting of work as a competition. Ask the students which assignments or projects they would like to have displayed.

✔ Post school goals lists and mission statements. These may reflect classroom, team, and/or school priorities.

✔ Display "thermometer graphs" to measure progress toward major class and/or school goals. Let students have responsibility for maintaining and posting changes in the "rising temperature." This makes for a changing and attractive center of attention involving the students themselves.

✔ Display maps, charts, graphs, and book jackets related to current and continuing study.

✔ Use student snapshots and polaroid photographs of the class members at school activities to create a bulletin board, collage, or montage for display.

Using Physical Space Effectively *(cont.)*

"On the Wall" Ideas *(cont.)*

✔ Post inspirational signs. There are many ways to help students believe in themselves. Take every opportunity to inspire and build their confidence. Short phrases or inspirational sayings can play a major role in this confidence-building process and foster a positive learning environment. Reproduce and display throughout your classroom some of the inspirational signs on page 23. You may even want to encourage your students to come up with some sayings of their own.

✔ Display numbers, letters, poems, songs, and sight words. These signs are key elements of the print-rich environment that whole-language advocates recommend.

✔ List monitor jobs and the students who are currently filling these roles. For the sake of efficiency, make sure the names on this list can be changed quickly and easily.

✔ Display posters, photographs, and other information relating to a unit being studied. These displays add valuable visual support to current topics.

✔ Post the Golden Rule.

✔ Create a visual representation of your classroom management system. The students will be more conscious of their behavior when they have something visual on which to focus.

✔ Create a class theme. Many teachers choose, or have their students choose, a year-long theme to tie their units of study together. Examples include "exploration" and "diversity."

✔ Use vowel and consonant cards. These are excellent for the primary grades. A vowel and consonant wall display serves as a learning and reinforcement tool for children. Some creative examples of how to display the short vowel sounds are presented on pages 20–22.

✔ Show home-school journals. You can hang these on the walls so you and the parents can have easy access to them.

✔ Post a list of the things students may do when they finish an assignment early.

✔ Try designing a mystery display board based on the popular game show Wheel of Fortune. Each week, offer a different class-related motto, famous saying, or appropriate epigram with only a few letters filled in to get the students started. Let students offer guesses for missing letters until one misses. At that point, suspend play until the next day when guessing may begin again, selecting a different student to start the game. When the puzzle is solved, leave the complete saying up for display and prepare a new mystery saying related to class study or school goals.

Vowel Cards

Vowels

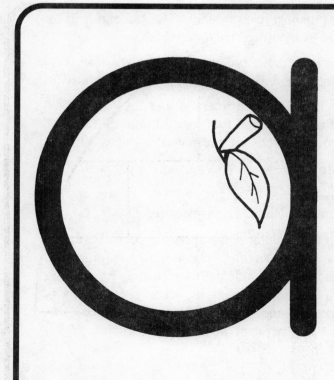 apple

20

Vowel Cards *(cont.)*

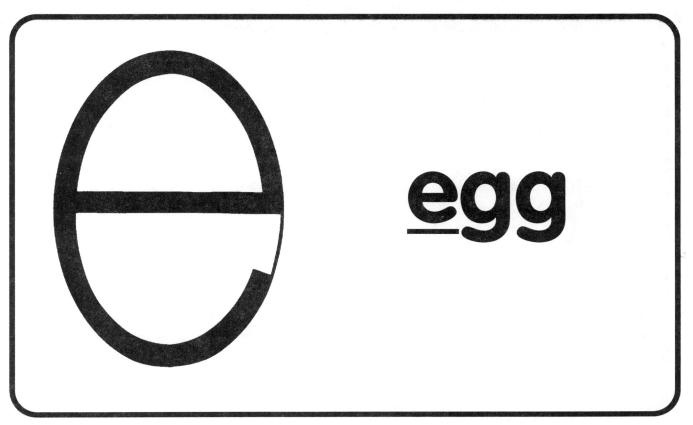

egg

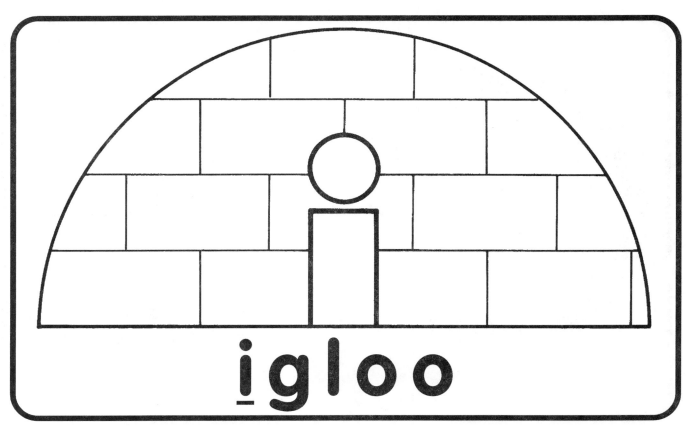

igloo

Vowel Cards (cont.)

Inspirational Signs

☆ Embrace challenges. ☆

☆ Find something good in every mistake. ☆

☆ Be your own best expert. ☆

☆ Turn weaknesses into strengths. ☆

☆ Be willing to work hard. ☆

☆ Refuse to accept limitations. ☆

☆ You can do it! ☆

☆ Be open to new ideas. ☆

☆ Always try your best. ☆

☆ Be your own best friend. ☆

☆ Tough times don't last; tough people do. ☆

☆ Think about succeeding every time. ☆

☆ The world needs you. ☆

☆ In anything you do, give it your best effort. ☆

☆ Don't ever give up. ☆

☆ Success = Talent + Knowledge x Attitude. ☆

☆ Rise above it. ☆

☆ Winners don't make excuses. ☆

☆ Never settle for second best. ☆

☆ Focus on improvement. ☆

Seating Arrangement

The configuration in which you arrange your students' desks can greatly facilitate or greatly impede learning. Traffic patterns, transitions, and cooperative learning activities are among the things that need to be considered when designing a seating configuration. While there are as many possible arrangements as there are teachers, the following suggestions should help all teachers arrange the items in their classrooms.

Seating Arrangement Tips

✔ Seat children in mixed-ability, gender, and ethnic groupings. While this is a sensitive area, it is important for the students to be integrated as thoroughly as possible.

✔ Arrange the students' desks in the configuration that you find most conducive to cooperative learning. This makes for smooth transitions between individual, group, and whole-class activities.

✔ Try to ensure that no students have their backs to the front of the room. If some do, have them turn their chairs and move into "listening position" whenever you are speaking in the front of the room so that they can see you as you speak.

✔ Do not be afraid to let friends sit next to each other. Since you are giving them the opportunity to do this, the students are responsible for making it work. If it does not work, you can always make a change.

✔ Allow plenty of space for foot traffic.

✔ Seat students away from items or areas that will distract them.

✔ Make sure that students with visual or hearing impairments sit near the front of the room.

✔ Make sure that no objects or displays impede any student's view to the front of the classroom.

✔ Some students may need to leave the room often or during lessons. Consider seating them near the back of the room so that their leaving does not distract the other students.

✔ Change the seating arrangement of your classroom every few months. Make sure that students who sit on the periphery of the class are brought into the center and vice versa. Some students do very well sitting in the center of the room yet cannot seem to focus when they are on the periphery of the classroom. The reverse is also true. Keep adjusting things until you find the configuration that works for the greatest number of your students.

Organizing Your Room

Teaching areas are those places where you gather students for instruction. It can be the whole class on a rug, a small group of 8–10 at a library table, or the whole class at their regular seats.

The subject or content area being taught, your style of teaching, and the needs of your students determine the teaching area you will use. You may also consider whether instruction is being done by cooperative learning groups, whole class direct instruction, small group instruction, or reteaching.

When setting up your room, you will want to have several kinds of teaching areas because at different times you will be using different types of instruction. When planning your room arrangement, consider how you want to be able to teach so that you will not have to rearrange the room to gather the students close to read them a story, or to share completed projects, give reports, etc.

When planning your room arrangement, avoid filling every space. There are times when you may want and need some open space for gathering students to use total body movement, to exercise during inclement weather, or to act out plays or puppet shows. If you have a rug, that area can be your open space. If you like your students to line up before leaving the room, remember to leave an area for that.

Seating Charts and Floor Plans

Use this checklist to indicate what requirements you will have when setting up your room arrangement and then create your own floor plan to meet your needs. A sample floor plan is provided on page 26. After you have decided on your floor plan, sketch it on a piece of 8½" x 11" paper and duplicate it several times. In pencil (so you can make adjustments) write student names where they will be assigned to work. If you team teach or teach by period, make a seating chart for each group of students. These charts will be very valuable when you have a substitute and also when changing seats.

☐ Bookshelves	☐ Library Tables	☐ Rug
☐ Television	☐ Centers	☐ Computer
☐ Teacher Desk	☐ Small-Group Instruction Area	☐ Coat Rack
☐ Supply Closet	☐ File Cabinet(s)	☐ Class Library
☐ Science Equipment	☐ Student Desks	☐ Display Table(s)

Sample Floor Plan

There is no rug area in this plan. It uses partner cooperative learning without moving furniture.

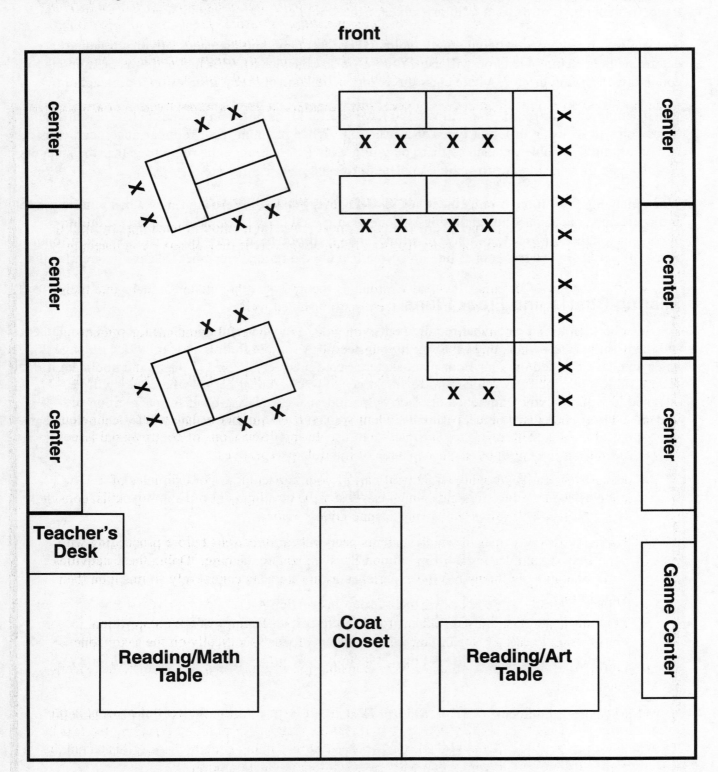

Modify floor plans to match available equipment and stationary furniture.

Developing Listening Skills

There are four main ways in which people use language: reading, writing, speaking, and listening. By far the most underdeveloped of these skills is that of listening. Attentive listening is important for two reasons. First, it is a demonstration of respect for the person speaking. Second, it is one of the major ways people learn new information. While teachers are often advised to improve the listening skills of their students, they are rarely shown how. The following suggestions will help you develop the listening skills of your students.

Ways to Develop Active Listeners

✔ Model attentive listening. Modeling is the most powerful method of teaching any skill to students. Students will be more likely to listen attentively if they observe you listening attentively.

✔ Praise attentive listening. Whenever students incorporate other student's ideas into their own statements, let them know that they really listened well.

✔ Read aloud to your students daily. Reading aloud is a powerful stimulant for students' imaginations and stretching their attention spans.

✔ Have a listening center in your classroom. Students can follow along in their books as they listen to tapes.

✔ During class discussions, before a student speaks, have him/her restate what the previous speaker said. This approach is effective to use during discussions of controversial issues because it may promote the acceptance of multiple perspectives.

✔ Make cooperative learning an integral part of your curriculum. For examples of cooperative learning strategies which can foster the development of listening skills, consult Susan Finney's *Together, I Can* and Jeanne Gibb's *Tribes.*

✔ Use activities or games in which students need to hear directions before proceeding with each step. Examples range from "Simon Says" to square dancing. Doing these activities with the lights out intensifies the experience as the students cannot rely so much on their visual sense.

✔ Play music and instruct the students to attend to certain features of the composition. During a piece of jazz, for instance, have students focus specifically on the saxophone.

✔ During oral reports have students be responsible for writing down 3–5 specific facts from each report.

✔ Make use of repeated or echo reading. Whichever term you use, the central concept is the same—The teacher reads a short passage, and the students respond by repeating the text in the same manner that the teacher read it. Besides promoting listening skills, this technique also helps students learn to read with greater inflection and emotion.

The Democratic Classroom

The future of our American democracy depends on the participation of our younger generations. Therefore, it is important that we make our classrooms as democratic as possible. If we train our students to take active, responsible roles in our classrooms now, then our society will be the better for it down the road.

Ways to Create a Democratic Classroom

✔ Allow students to help develop the class rules, rewards, and consequences.

✔ Simulate adult democratic practices. Organize a mock trial to allow students to experience what it is like to sit on a jury, encourage students to write letters to their congressmen and senators, or try to arrange field trips to city council or school board meetings.

✔ Put a suggestion box in your classroom.

✔ Allow students to discuss and vote on major class issues. Students, for example, could vote on which work they would like to have displayed in the classroom, or they could decide upon a class theme which you could use to tie together the different topics you study.

✔ Teach students to value one another's opinion. This can be done by modeling, praising, and raising the consciousness of effective listening. Please see the list entitled, "Ways to Develop Active Listeners" (page 27).

✔ Hold class elections. Try to structure the election campaign in a manner similar to real life campaigns. Include components such as debates, position papers, and voter registration.

✔ During class discussions allow the current speaker to select the next speaker. When you employ this method of selecting speakers, you are allowing students to share power and responsibility.

✔ Teach students to use basic parliamentary procedure regarding opening and closing meetings, calling on members to speak, and holding elections for offices or deciding on major class issues. Have students take turns serving as chairperson.

The Democratic Classroom *(cont.)*

Ways to Create a Democratic Classroom *(cont.)*

✔ Develop leadership qualities in students. Too often, the ability to act as a leader is seen as a quality with which one either is or is not born. Not appreciated is the fact that many of our great leaders did not always demonstrate leadership potential and had to grow into their roles. Leadership is a quality all children can develop, and the classroom can be a wonderful training ground for our society's future leaders. Suggested ways to develop leadership qualities in students are provided on page 30.

✔ Have students, either alone or in groups, teach material to the class. This is another way in which students learn to take responsibility for what occurs in the classroom.

✔ Have students create their own tests. Ask each student to submit to you five possible test questions from which you incorporate at least one question from each person into the test.

✔ Put a problem pail in your classroom. This gives students a discreet way and place to alert you to any problems that may be occurring in the classroom.

✔ Allow students to have the right to pass when taking turns in a group discussion. Such a right gives students a sense of freedom and a sense of control. The right to pass, a core component of Jeanne Gibb's *Tribes* program, remains in effect only in situations where students are sharing their personal opinions and feelings. It should not be used by students as a way of avoiding responsibility for school work.

✔ Co-construct the curriculum along with your students. To the extent that you are comfortable, let the interests of the students drive what your class studies. Student motivation will dramatically increase when the curriculum comes from them.

✔ Organize a mock student congress to write bills and bring them to the floor for amendment, passage, or denial. Bills may be serious, covering controversial topics like cigarette advertising, as well as humorous, such as those proposing laws banning homework on special T.V. nights. This is an ideal opportunity for small group/large group interaction—democracy at work. The activity promotes creative thought, cooperation, speaking skills, self-confidence, and knowledge of democratic debate and legislation.

✔ Organize club activities. As voluntary student-directed and interest-generated activities, these become primary centers of democratic behavior originating in the classroom. The students thereby share in the direction and growth of their own abilities—a powerful stimulus to self-confidence and democratic self-rule.

Ways to Develop Leadership Skills

✔ Discuss the question, "Are people born leaders, or can individuals be trained or taught to be leaders?"

✔ Discuss the qualities of famous leaders.

✔ Praise students who display leadership in daily classroom or playground situations.

✔ Discuss the areas in which leadership can be shown.

✔ Discuss the moral obligations of leadership.

✔ Allow students to gain practice as leaders by providing opportunities for them in role-playing situations, cooperative group activities, and classroom monitor responsibilities.

✔ Discuss different styles of leadership. These include, but are not limited to, leading by example and leading vocally.

✔ Organize mentorships with community leaders for your students.

✔ Invite community leaders to speak to your class.

✔ Encourage students to read biographies.

✔ Encourage students to interview community leaders.

✔ Discuss why we need leaders in our society.

✔ Teach and allow your students to practice various subskills associated with leadership. Most notably, these include persuasive speaking and effective listening.

Providing Individual Attention

Children enjoy and develop from the individual attention they receive from role models. With increasing class sizes, however, it has become more difficult to provide this type of attention to each and every student. This list will help you find ways to relate more personally with your students. Even a few minutes a week of extra attention can make a world of difference to your students. Following are specific ways to provide individual attention to students.

Ways to Individualize Attention

✔ Circulate while students are working independently. Make it a goal to converse meaningfully with every student as you circulate.

✔ Randomly select a "Student of the Week" to feature on a bulletin board. To boost the self-esteem of the Student of the Week, sit him/her on a special chair and have the other students take turns saying what they like about that student. Record these statements and post them on a bulletin board along with a "Student of the Week" certificate, a picture of that student, and a sample of that student's work. For a variation of this idea, please see the insert (page 33) which follows this list.

✔ Send a positive note or postcard home to a student whenever you have the slightest reason to do so. You may want to have the students address a few postcards at the beginning of the year so that they will be ready at hand for you. Sending a positive note home with a student after he/she has done something particularly well or has tried particularly hard can be a powerful morale booster.

✔ Maintain interactive journals with students so that you can communicate on a frequent, confidential basis. Reserving a few moments at the end of each school day for students to make entries into these journals is a good way to regularize this practice.

✔ Have lunch with a student every once in a while. Don't just talk about work. Be personal. Ask about their hobbies and after-school activities.

✔ Praise students privately to their friends who will relay the news, doubling its effectiveness when the recipient realizes you appreciate him or her and also knows that the friend now realizes it too.

✔ Ask a student privately to do a favor for you or provide a bit of help—something you will be grateful for. It need not be a major matter, but it directs a bit of personal and individual recognition to one who may not have felt that touch before. Asking another for help often provides that person with a strong feeling of worth. Consider one of the major intangibles of teaching—the silent reward of knowing one has been able to help another.

Providing Individual Attention *(cont.)*

Ways to Individualize Attention *(cont.)*

✔ Invite students to attend parent conferences.

✔ Have periodic teacher-student conferences. These can be arranged whenever you need to discuss something with the student, whether it be academic or personal in nature.

✔ Consider making a home visit to each of your students.

✔ Send a personal letter to each student before the school year begins, expressing how much you are looking forward to having him/her in your class.

✔ Watch students participate in extra-curricular activities such as Little League games or musical performances.

✔ Provide opportunities for students to share objects, stories, or ideas of meaning to them. You can either do this as a sponge activity whenever you have a few minutes here or there, or you can schedule a daily or weekly sharing time. Sharing time allows students to be the center of attention while also giving them the chance to feel like experts about whatever they are discussing.

✔ Whenever you have a few extra minutes, ask your students to volunteer to say something kind about another student or the entire class.

✔ Initiate a "Reading Buddy" Program with another classroom. In a Reading Buddy Program a class of upper-grade students works one-on-one with a class of primary students to improve the latter's reading skills. The older children experience the feeling of being needed and appreciated while the younger students benefit from the assistance and undivided attention of older friends. A sample Reading Buddy Program Letter appears on page 96. Feel free to expand this activity to include activities other than reading. Please see the following page for a notice to be sent home, containing information about how parents, teachers, and Reading Buddies can help younger partners develop self-confidence through a weekly VIP (Very Important Person) activity program.

Very Important Person

Dear _____,

Each week a student in our class will be a Very Important Person (or VIP) for the week. He or she will decorate a bulletin board in a way that will reflect his or her accomplishments, interests, and family. A profile sheet, "I Am Proud to Be Me," should be completed and used in the presentation. Your child will put up a display on the first day of your week.

_____ will *be*

the Very Important Person for the week of_____.

Here are some ideas:

- certificates, awards
- a baby picture
- current pictures of yourself
- pictures of the family
- pictures or drawings of you doing things you like to do
- a paper telling your "favorites": food, subject, book, singer, movie, friend, color, sport, hobby, etc.
- trophies
- a favorite toy or belonging
- a story or poem you wrote
- a paper you are proud of

As an example, I started the year with a bulletin board of me, and I had great fun putting it all together. I encourage parents to help their child in choosing and finding things for their bulletin board.

Sincerely,

_____

Discussion Time

Class discussions are wonderful forums for sharing opinions, clarifying values, and imparting information. If not handled properly, they can also open the door for behavior problems and periods of inattentiveness. The following tips will help make these occasions function more smoothly.

Tips for a Smooth Discussion

✔ Establish a signal. A short, predetermined audible and/or visual signal such as "Eyes on me!" or blinking the lights alerts students to the fact that you need their attention immediately.

✔ Stand in front of the room when talking to the students, but circulate throughout the room frequently. Students' attentiveness will increase, and disruptions will be kept to a minimum when your students know you are keeping a close eye on them.

✔ Before asking students to raise their hands to contribute to a discussion or to answer a question, give them a few seconds to ponder the question and process their thoughts. This prevents your discussions from becoming races in which the quicker-thinking students always dominate.

✔ Be sure to call on students seated throughout the room, not just from one area. This is a matter of fairness as well as an effective way to maintain the attention of all the students.

✔ Dignify every student response. Doing this establishes that the contributions of every student are valuable and worthy of attention.

✔ Do not publicly compare the performance or behavior of students. *The authors feel very strongly about this point.* This practice leads to unhealthy competition among students and severely damages the self-esteem of many.

✔ Keep a graphic record of individual oral participation. One way to do this is to keep a transparent overlay on your seating chart. Record check strokes for each student's participation in a given discussion. These can be wiped away at the end of each session and transferred to a permanent chart. A graphic picture of discussion participation will emerge as time goes on. You will then be able to encourage those who have been reticent and call on those you have overlooked. This is a very instructive tool, often letting a teacher know how some students may be consistently overlooked in class discussions.

✔ A variation of this procedure is to maintain a class discussion chart with students taking turns at recording and maintaining the flow of discussion. Care must be taken here to prevent public comparison of individual students, a destructive practice in most cases.

Discussion Time *(cont.)*

Tips for a Smooth Discussion *(cont.)*

✔ Make it clear to students that their hands need to be held high if they wish to be recognized. It is often unclear whether a student is raising a hand or merely stretching. This suggestion helps avoid any uncertainty.

✔ Teach students to value one another's opinions. Students should listen attentively to their classmates because it is a show of respect and because they learn a great deal of useful information.

✔ Model effective listening and praise it in others.

✔ Allow students to have the right to pass during a class discussion. The right to pass helps students gain a sense of control over their own behavior. One of the "Four Norms" of Jeanne Gibbs' *Tribes* program, the right to pass, applies only to situations where students are sharing their feelings or opinions. Teachers must not allow their students to invoke the right to pass as a way to avoid being held accountable for school work.

✔ After a student finishes speaking, allow that student to select the next speaker in the discussion. This practice gives students an opportunity to learn how to share power responsibly.

✔ Distribute turns equitably during discussions or activities in which all students wish to participate. An efficient way to accomplish this is to write each student's name on a craft stick and place all the sticks in a cup. Then, whenever you need to select a student to speak, pick one stick out of the cup at random, and the student whose name is on it receives a turn. Once a student's stick has been selected, remove it from the cup until all others have been selected. Then, place all the sticks back into the cup.

✔ Emphasize that only one person can speak at a time for a productive discussion to occur. Many teachers employ a "talking rock" or "talking ball" into their class discussions to reinforce this point. Only the person who is holding the object has the right to speak.

How to. . .

Effectively Manage
the
Classroom

36

Developing a Management System

Effective classroom management is a necessary precondition for productive learning. While we as teachers would much rather spend our time focusing on the more creative aspects of teaching, it is important to have a well-designed classroom management system. The following suggestions will help you in this area.

Practical Tips for Classroom Management

✔ Construct a hierarchy of consequences, from the least to the most severe, so that students know what happens to them each time they break a rule. There is no need to feel constrained by this system. For example, if a first rule violation is very serious, do not hesitate to proceed right to the top of this hierarchy.

✔ Post classroom standards, rewards, and consequences so they are visible. If they are in sight, they are more likely to be in the students' minds.

✔ Model the very behaviors you expect your students to demonstrate. You must be consistent in your words and deeds.

✔ Treat each child as you would like to be treated and encourage your students to do the same.

✔ Have students brainstorm and vote on the class rules. This gives them a sense of ownership over what occurs in the classroom.

✔ Role play inevitable problem-causing situations before they happen so that students can gain practice in solving them.

✔ Invest ample time early in the school year to clarify and reinforce the class rules. While it may seem like wasted time now, you will save an enormous amount of time in the future.

✔ Never cause a child to lose dignity. This is one of Madeline Hunter's major points. For further information about her pioneering work in the area of classroom management, please consult *Discipline That Develops Self-Discipline.*

Developing a Management System *(cont.)*

Practical Tips for Classroom Management *(cont.)*

✔ Be flexible enough to add or delete rules as needed throughout the year.

✔ Use the principal only as a very last resort when disciplining. Exhaust all your internal management options before resorting to external ones.

✔ Emphasize and reinforce the importance of saying "please" and "thank you."

✔ Make negative behavior promote positive action if possible. When disciplining a student, for example, try saying something like, "You are too good a person to be behaving this way." This approach acknowledges the inappropriate behavior while simultaneously building up the child's self-esteem.

✔ Catch the students being good. This technique suggests that teachers call attention to students who are behaving properly instead of focusing on those behaving improperly. Even if only one student is doing what you have asked, praising that one student strongly will slowly but consistently produce a snowball effect, drawing all the students into productive behavior patterns.

✔ Give full disciplinary authority to your aide and parent volunteers. Emphasize to the students that they are expected to regard classroom helpers as extensions of you and to treat them with the same respect.

✔ Look for opportunities to put disruptive, talkative, or "antsy" students in positions where they can help others so that they will feel needed and will not distract the class.

✔ Try not to threaten, but if you do, follow through on it. Your credibility is perhaps your greatest asset. You will maintain it by delivering on your promises.

✔ When settling a disciplinary matter, take the least intrusive step possible. During a lesson, for example, do not punish a mischievous student when a simple glance his or her way will achieve the same result. Taking such a step will save your time, preserve your patience, and maintain the cohesiveness of your lesson.

✔ While you are circulating around the room and helping students who are doing independent seatwork, always position yourself so that you can see the entire class at a glance. By frequently looking around the room, you teach your students that they will not be permitted to drift off task or to distract others.

Developing a Management System *(cont.)*

Practical Tips for Classroom Management *(cont.)*

✔ Do not publicly compare the performance or behavior of individual students. *The authors feel very strongly about this point.* This practice leads to unhealthy competition among students and severely damages the self-esteem of many.

✔ To build both a sense of independence as well as a spirit of cooperation when students are doing seatwork, require them to pose all questions to someone at their table before they can pose them to you.

✔ Be consistent in enforcing rules. Except for severe offenses, one warning is often a good idea before applying a specific consequence for a rule violation. After one warning, the consequence should invariably follow.

✔ Often a brief and courteous admonition written on a sticky note and placed on a student's desk will redirect a talkative or dreamy child's attention back to the subject at hand. This is silent and does not draw other's attention to the individual. The teacher can quietly place it on the student's desk while walking by. An offending student will often respond positively to a reminder that does not publicly call attention to him or her. A quiet smile from the teacher will do much to punctuate the note when the student looks up.

✔ Humor, if appropriately used, can be very effective in classroom management. In general, it should be applied quietly and with individuals for maximum effectiveness. A shared joke can bond a teacher and student in a friendly relationship that can be lasting. Sarcasm, no matter how humorous it might appear at the time, should never be directed toward students. One can never really gauge the lasting hurt a cutting remark may make in a child.

Guiding Principles

It is very easy to get lost in the details of teaching. Every once in a while, it is necessary to step back and focus on the bigger picture. At these times, we need to remember the larger ideas which form the basis of our teaching philosophy. In short, we need to remind ourselves of the principles that guide us. These principles form the basis of a well-managed classroom in which students have a sense of purpose, are eager to learn, and take pride in their accomplishments.

Principles to Remember

✔ Teach and model every action you expect your students to be able to perform. This point applies to a wide variety of actions, ranging from sharpening pencils to handwriting words to treating others kindly.

✔ Hold students responsible for the messes they create.

✔ Do not do anything for students that they can do for themselves. After all, a teacher's job is to empower students to become independent learners. While students are working at their desks, for example, before they come to you with questions, require them to ask everyone at their table first.

✔ Hold students accountable for their own learning. Accountability means that students face consequences whenever their performance does not rise to the level of your expectations.

✔ Emphasize the value and uniqueness of every child.

✔ Remember that students learn in various ways. There is no one learning style. Some students learn best by seeing (visual learners), others by hearing (auditory learners), and others by doing (kinesthetic learners). It is important to impart information and develop skills in ways that cater to these various learning styles.

✔ Stress all four modes of language. To develop language skills, students must be reading, writing, speaking, and listening on a regular basis.

✔ There are multiple intelligences. Traditionally, educators have recognized and acknowledged only two kinds of intelligence—verbal and mathematical. Howard Gardner, a Harvard researcher, has identified seven intelligences which he argues must be developed on an individual basis.

✔ Ask higher-order questions on a regular basis. In today's global economy, basic skills are not enough. Citizens need to be able to perform higher-order thinking skills such as analyzing, comparing, and evaluating information.

Guiding Principles *(cont.)*

Principles to Remember *(cont.)*

✔ Make curricular material meaningful to students. If your students find meaning in your curriculum, their motivation will be greater and their understanding will be deeper.

✔ Allow a great deal of student choice in your classroom. This will also increase student motivation.

✔ Teach the whole child. Strive to develop the cognitive, affective, and psychomotor domains of all of your students.

✔ Set students up for success. Assignments should be neither too difficult nor too easy. If students put forth the effort, then success should be attainable.

✔ The best way to solve problems is to prevent them from occurring. Students should have the opportunities early in the school year to role play potentially difficult situations so that they will be able to handle them as they arise later in the year.

✔ Focus on the things students can do and build on those. It is focusing on what these students can do and proceeding from there that often allows you to give these students their best chances for success.

✔ Catch the students being good. This expression reminds teachers to recognize and reinforce good behavior, no matter how hard it may be to find sometimes, instead of focusing on examples of poor behavior. Even if only one student does what you have asked, praise that student strongly; slowly but surely, the other students will follow along on the right path.

✔ Capitalize on curiosity. Find out what the student wants to know and let that be the guide to how you present individual lessons in math, social studies, etc.

✔ Tap the power of group support with total class projects designed for success—charity drives, community improvement, school beautification, etc.

✔ Involve everyone in the search for success in all activities. For every activity, design specific learning facts from the curriculum—mathematics, geography, science, language, etc., that can be measured and mastered.

Class Mission

There is an old saying, "If you don't know where you're going, you can never get there." This adage applies directly to teaching. We as teachers need to know what we hope to accomplish with our students before we can set about doing it. A class mission statement created by you and your students offers one way for your class to appreciate exactly what your goals are during your precious time together. The following are some elements which your class may wish to include in your mission statement.

Elements of a Class Mission Statement

✔ For all students to feel safe and comfortable being themselves.

✔ For all students to feel encouraged to participate.

✔ For all students to tolerate mistakes and view them as opportunities for learning.

✔ For all students to become active, effective listeners. (Please see the list entitled "Ways to Develop Active Listeners" on page 27.)

✔ For all students to take charge of and become responsible for their own behavior and their own learning.

✔ For all students to learn to love learning.

✔ For all students to realize how important education is for their futures.

✔ For all students to see themselves as part of a classroom community, a community where we help and encourage one another.

✔ For all students to realize the value of hard work and perseverance.

✔ For all students to have respect for themselves and others.

✔ For all students to respect and appreciate the differences both among the students in the class and among the people of the world.

✔ For all students to acknowledge their strengths and weaknesses.

✔ For all students to strive toward continuous improvement.

✔ For all students to believe in themselves and to realize that the sky is the limit for every one of them.

Morning Activities

The morning activities set the tone for the rest of the day. Taking attendance is one of these activities which can help create a positive tone. This activity can be looked at it in one of two ways, either as a mundane task which needs to be done as quickly and painlessly as possible or as a learning opportunity. The next list contains some ways of taking attendance that will appeal to teachers of both mindsets.

Ways to Take Attendance

✔ Say "Good Morning" to each student individually in a foreign language as the students work on an assignment at their desks. You can choose a different language each week.

✔ Have a daily sign-in sheet for the students as they enter the room.

✔ Have students turn a personalized attendance card over from one color to another as soon as they enter the class and quickly see whose cards have not been turned over.

✔ Have a student monitor in charge of taking attendance visually.

✔ You, a student monitor, or your aide can visually take attendance.

✔ Have students take an object off a table. See how many are left on the table after everyone has taken one, and as a class, determine who is absent.

✔ Call out each student's name and have each respond by stating one thing learned from yesterday. (See the list on page 45, "Methods of Excusing Students" for some other ideas along this same line.)

✔ Call out each student's name and have each respond by turning in the homework. This takes care of two tasks at the same time.

✔ Have cooperative groups be responsible for taking attendance within each of their groups, and then designate one person from each group to relay this information to you.

✔ Make an attendance graph. On one column, include the students who are present and on the other, those who are absent. You can even create an equation or a word problem from this data.

The Morning Routine

A morning routine is very important for establishing consistency in your classroom. When students arrive each day, they will settle into the day much more smoothly when they know exactly what they should be doing. Here are some ideas which you might choose to incorporate into your morning routine.

Elements of a Morning Routine

✔ Use a sponge activity. When the students first enter the room, have them respond on paper to a prompt that you have written on the board. (Please refer to the sponge activities list on page 60 for some examples of possible prompts.) When your students see one of these prompts on the board, they know that they must get seated quickly if they are to have enough time to finish the activity.

✔ Change the calendar. For the primary grades, changing the calendar is a wonderful time to introduce, extend, or review basic math concepts. For more information, please consult Mary Baratta-Lorton's *Mathematics Their Way.*

✔ Take attendance.

✔ Take lunch count. Determine how many students are eating in the cafeteria.

✔ Recite a pledge. Your school district may require the Pledge of Allegiance, or you may wish to use one created by the students to either the school or to one another.

✔ Preview the schedule for the day.

✔ Discuss information the students may need regarding upcoming school events or activities. Examples include reports, field trips, or special class projects.

✔ Include a "This Day in History" feature in which you discuss a major happening which occurred on that same day of an earlier year.

✔ Discuss current events.

✔ Announce the names of the new monitors and the new Student of the Week. You will probably only need to do this once a week or once every two weeks.

✔ Copy and/or read the morning message off the board. This message can pertain to any information you feel the class needs to know.

✔ Play "Categories." This is a brief game in which you present three objects or items, and the students have to guess the category to which they all belong, thus developing higher-level thinking skills of generalization. For example, bananas, apples, and oranges are all fruits.

Dismissing Students

Usually, teachers dismiss students to go to recess, lunch, or elsewhere by calling individual names or tables. Excusing students by various other criteria besides their name or table is an enjoyable activity that produces academic as well as motivational benefits. By starting the excusing process with the direction of "Be thinking of your favorite . . ." or other such phrase, the students continue using their brains instead of coasting into the next activity. When the teacher calls that birthday month, clothing color, favorite cookie, etc., the students wearing those colors or thinking of those cookies are dismissed. In addition, this method promotes a sense of individuality as well as being a change of pace while still being orderly.

Methods of Excusing Students

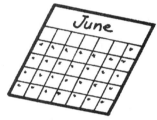

Be thinking of your . . .
Birthday month
Clothing colors
Favorite animal
Favorite color
Favorite cookie
Favorite day of the week
Favorite dessert
Favorite flower
Favorite ice cream flavor
Favorite food
Favorite drink
Favorite fruit
Favorite pizza
Favorite season
Favorite sport
Favorite type of music
Favorite vegetable
Favorite occupation
Type of pets

Rewards

Rewarding students when they perform or behave well shows them that their conduct has been noticed. In addition, rewarding students' behavior increases the likelihood that such behavior will be repeated in the future. While there are many different theories about which type of rewards to give, we believe that intangible ones are the best kind. Tangible rewards can lead to problems. Too often, they become a crutch and resemble bribes. Inevitably, whenever students who have grown accustomed to tangible rewards are asked to do something, they will ask what is in it for them.

Intangible rewards based on the ideas of choice and freedom do not present these same types of problems.

Whichever type of rewards you choose, however, it is vitally important for students to understand that they are expected to behave well because it is the right thing to do, not because they are going to get something for it. It is not necessary to reward students every time they behave or perform well. At first, it is a good idea to reward students frequently so that good habits become ingrained. After a while, decrease the frequency of rewards until you reach the point where you can use them at the most judicious and opportune times.

Intangible Rewards

Praise—A teacher's kind words show students that they are competent, worthy of recognition, and valued for the effort they put forth. It is difficult to overestimate the power of this simple act. Moreover, it is especially effective with shy students and those whose work commonly falls into the "average" category. Such students are rarely admonished for anything negative, but neither are they recognized for accomplishment. (It is the obstreperous, the aggressive, and the academically gifted who usually garner the teacher's attention.) Consciously try to praise those students who have not been recognized before; then watch for some good results. Let your praise find its way to the home through a personal note to parents; then watch your students' confidence blossom and competence grow.

Those who doubt the effectiveness of praise in the classroom need only consider how well it works on the job—in schools as well as in private business.

Choice of monitor job—If students are allowed to choose their own responsibilities, their motivation will increase and their performance will improve.

Free time—This allows time to do whatever the student wishes as long as it does not disturb other students.

Rewards *(cont.)*

Intangible Rewards *(cont.)*

Homework pass—This may be redeemable for one night free from homework.

Student of the Week—Many teachers choose to reward a hard-working student by naming him/her the Student of the Week.

Early dismissal to recess or lunch—Even a one-minute headstart means a great deal to children.

Lunch with the teacher—This is a great way for a teacher to provide individual attention to students in an informal setting.

Unit-based rewards—Here, the teacher finds a way to benefit a student's progress during a class unit. For example, suppose the students have a $10 budget with which to run a country in a government unit. If one student is behaving exceptionally well, reward that student by increasing his/her budget to $11.

Good note/phone call home—To have maximum impact, this message should be delivered as soon as possible after the behavior which prompted it. Be sure to let the parent know exactly what the student did that was so commendable.

Teacher's special helper—Choose someone to assist you whenever a special chore not covered by one of the other monitor jobs needs to be done.

Participation in special project—Many teachers create projects in which only those who have performed or behaved well may participate.

An opportunity to help write the weekly class newsletter—This weekly correspondence will often have more meaning for parents if it is at least partly written by students.

Choice of seating position—If students choose where they will sit, they will have more of a stake in taking responsibility for their performance there.

Choice of the book you will read aloud for story time—This empowers the students, concurrently supporting the implication that reading and its joys are much to be desired.

Coupons redeemable for various privileges—These privileges might be extra computer time, being able to read outside the classroom, being able to play a special game, or a trip to the class library. Please see the insert which follows this list for some sample coupon designs.

Coupon Patterns

Establishing Classroom Rules

Rules provide structure and define limits so that students know what behavior will be acceptable in your classroom. Rules also offer an element of safety. Whichever rules you and/or the students decide to adopt for your classroom, make sure that each is clearly explained and modeled and that the students have the chance to practice each one. Try not to have too many rules, however, since having a large number of rules dilutes the impact of each one.

Finally, feel free to add or subtract rules throughout the year as needed. The following list contains some rules which you and your class may find beneficial.

Classroom Rules

✔ No talking when the teacher is talking.

✔ Stay seated. This rule prevents students from wandering around the room whenever they like.

✔ Stay working. When students finish assignments early, this rule reminds them that they are expected to stay productively occupied. (Please see the list on page 59 entitled, "Things for Students to Do When They Finish Assignments Early.")

✔ Follow directions.

✔ Listen attentively.

✔ Do not complain.

✔ Do not tattle. Students need to be shown the difference between reporting (the sharing of vital information) and tattling (merely attempting to get one another in trouble.)

✔ Have respect for others. This rule encompasses listening to others, having respect for people's feelings, and treating other people's property as you would your own.

✔ Look for ways to make this class a better place. This is an intentionally ambiguous rule which allows room for students to define positive action in their own terms.

✔ Raise your hand when you would like a turn to speak. This prevents students from calling out answers when it is not their turn.

✔ Do not belittle anyone. This is to prevent put-downs, sarcasms, or other demeaning remarks.

✔ Do not interfere in anyone else's learning. This is another general rule incorporating a wide variety of behavior.

Establishing Classroom Consequences

Whichever rules you and/or your class ultimately decide to adopt, they will have the desired effect only when they are backed up by meaningful, logical consequences. The most effective consequences are based on the ideas of loss of freedom and loss of time. For example, the simple axiom "If you take the class's time, I am going to take your time" works very well. To save yourself the time and frustration of having to enforce the rules all throughout the year, spend the necessary time at the beginning of the year to make sure your expectations are clear. You will be glad you did.

Many teachers choose approximately four consequences and organize them into a series of steps so that the consequences become more severe with each rule violation. Other teachers focus instead on whole-class consequences, such as keeping the whole class inside for part of recess. These teachers believe that focusing on the whole class encourages students to take responsibility for helping one another. Whatever your beliefs are, we hope the following list contains some examples of consequences that you will find helpful.

Meaningful Consequences

Loss of part or all of recess—Students sit in the classroom with their heads down on their desks, thinking about how they can behave better in the future.

Loss of opportunity to serve as a monitor—With this as a consequence, monitor jobs, and thus the opportunity to take responsibility in the classroom, will be more coveted.

Note or phone call home—Few students relish the idea of disapproval from both teacher and parent.

After-school detention—Loss of precious after-school free time is a dreaded thought to most youngsters.

Behavior contract—For the teacher and student to sign, this contract spells out the specific behavior to be changed, an appropriate replacement behavior, a reward which will be provided upon successful completion of the contract, and a timetable. (For more information, see Madeline Hunter's *Discipline That Develops Self-Discipline*).

Time-out/Put head down—A few minutes to settle down often helps students regain their poise.

Public apology to class—This is a somewhat controversial idea, but many feel such a step increases group cohesion and identification.

Loss of participation—Missing out on field trips or special class activities such as birthday or holiday parties is not something students look forward to.

A Positive Classroom Atmosphere

One key component to a productive classroom is a positive classroom atmosphere. The relationship between a positive classroom atmosphere and classroom management does not always receive the attention it deserves.

The feeling which exists in a classroom to a large extent determines the productivity of the students in it. Children operating within an atmosphere of trust, mutual respect, and positivity are likely to focus their energies on becoming effective learners. In contrast, students encountering an environment of suspicion, disrespect, and negativity are not likely to develop their full intellectual potential. In addition, where students feel included, appreciated, and valued, discipline problems are unlikely to emerge. Common sense tells us that happy students should have no reason to rock the boat.

Because of this important link between a positive atmosphere, classroom management, and academic performance, it is vital for teachers to do all that they can in order to create a positive feeling in their classrooms. The following suggestions should help you in this endeavor.

Adding a Positive Atmosphere

✔ Treat each child as you would like to be treated and encourage your students to do the same. The Golden Rule is always an excellent thought to keep in mind.

✔ Seize every opportunity to remind your class that each student is unique and special.

✔ Whenever you have a few free minutes, ask your students to volunteer to say something kind about another student or the class as a whole.

✔ Laugh with your students.

✔ Each morning make your first contact with each student a positive one. No matter how rushed you are, offer a "Good morning" or a "How are you" before proceeding with class business.

✔ Say "Please" and "Thank you" every chance you get. You will be amazed at how quickly this behavior spreads.

A Positive Classroom Atmosphere *(cont.)*

Adding a Positive Atmosphere *(cont.)*

✔ Provide opportunities for your students to share personally meaningful objects or news with the whole class. You can either set aside a few moments each day for this or designate a special time each week.

✔ Let students know you appreciate the effort they put forth. Everybody likes to be recognized for his or her hard work.

✔ Covertly or overtly, point out instances of individual student improvement to your whole class.

✔ Avoid publicly comparing the academic performance or behavior of the students in your class. Comments of this nature develop feelings of ill will, jealousy, and inferiority among your students.

✔ Prevent the academic or behavioral difficulties of one student from becoming the business of the whole class. Students will appreciate the fact that you respect their privacy.

✔ When displaying the work of your students, display the work of all your students.

✔ Do everything possible to build a sense of inclusion in your classroom. If you have not already, please consult the book *Tribes* for some valuable ideas as to how to accomplish this goal.

✔ Incorporate music into your classroom routine whenever possible.

✔ Be on the lookout for students who may be having a rough day academically or socially and try to find some way to give them a boost. Your students will appreciate your concern. Two steps you might take to give a student a boost are allowing that student to choose his/her favorite monitor job and allowing that student to be the next Student of the Week. (For more information about the Student of the Week idea, please see the list on page 31.)

✔ Make negative behavior promote positive action if possible. When disciplining a student, for example, try saying something like, "You are too good a person to be behaving this way." This approach acknowledges the inappropriate behavior while simultaneously building up the child's self-esteem.

✔ Catch the students being good. First suggested in Guiding Principles on page 41, this technique suggests that teachers call attention to students who are behaving properly instead of focusing on those behaving improperly. Even if only one student is doing what you have asked, praising that one student strongly will slowly but consistently produce a snowball effect, drawing all the students into a productive behavior pattern.

Classroom Responsibilities

It is important to allow your students to assume increasing amounts of responsibility over class procedures. Trusting students to fulfill various duties builds independence and increases self-esteem. Students enjoy their roles as monitors and take them seriously. You can either rotate monitor jobs randomly or use them to reward students who demonstrate good behavior. When the need arises during the year for a new monitor, do not hesitate to create a new title. In addition, we suggest that you change monitors every week or two and feel free to combine separate monitor jobs into one title if the need arises.

Finally, it is important to allow students of both genders to perform every type of job so that you do not unwittingly reinforce any gender stereotypes.

Monitors

Door—This student opens and closes the doors and controls the lights whenever the class leaves or enters the room.

Paper/Materials—This student collects from and distributes supplies to students at their desks.

Sports Equipment—This student carries sports equipment out to P.E. or recess.

Pencil—This student sharpens pencils at recess for students who need this service done. This task is done at recess so that the sharpener noise does not bother busy students.

Library—This student makes sure all overdue books are returned.

Line Leader—This student has the responsibility of keeping his/her line straight and quiet.

Attendance—This student takes attendance each morning either orally or visually. Please see "Ways to Take Attendance" on page 43.

Book Set—This student is responsible for distributing and collecting all classroom sets of books that are not checked out individually.

Science Equipment—This student is responsible for distributing, storing, and cataloguing any equipment used at desks or learning centers. This includes such items as magnets, lenses, scales, thermometers, microscopes, etc.

Window—This student is responsible for opening and closing windows at the beginning and end of the day, along with controlling shades or blinds.

A-V—This student is responsible for maintaining and operating projectors, tape recorders, and video equipment.

Technology—This student is responsible for storing and distributing computer-related materials such as disks, CD ROM, etc. In some cases this monitor can become skilled in helping other students with computer operation.

Classroom Responsibilities

Monitors *(cont.)*

Lunch Cards/Lunch Money—This student distributes lunch cards to some students and holds lunch money for other students.

Office—This student travels to the office to deliver or receive messages.

Room-to-Room—This student travels to other rooms whenever a message needs to be delivered. This job can be combined with the office monitor's to become the "messenger" monitor.

Clean-Up—This student supervises classroom clean-up sessions.

Team Captain—This student is responsible for leading a team during P.E.

Calendar/Date—This student changes the calendar each month and changes the date on the board each day.

Chalkboard—This student erases the board at the teacher's request.

Eraser—This student cleans the erasers outside the class at the teacher's request.

Music—This student turns radio/stereo/record player on and off at teacher's request.

Correspondence—This student writes and sends thank-you notes or any other necessary correspondence.

Tattle-Tale Monitor—Choose one student to whom all the others are to go when they feel the need to tattle on someone. This monitor screens these tattles and reports the serious incidents to you.

Wastebasket—This monitor empties the wastebaskets whenever they become full.

Lunch Bench—This student oversees the lunch area to make sure that all the trash is picked up and that all the tables and benches are clean.

Pet—This student takes care of any pets you might have in your classroom.

Classroom Contingencies

Unexpected situations seem to occur all the time. Though it is impossible to plan for them all in advance, it is wise to try to gain a sense of control over them. The following list contains suggestions for handling some of the most common contingencies. Your stress level will be greatly reduced if you have thought of clear, simple procedures for dealing with each one before they ever actually happen.

Planning for Contingencies

✔ Assemble a packet of assignments for each day's absent students. Have one folder or area where you can put all necessary work, instructions, and notices. The insert on page 56 offers you one possible way to organize assignments.

✔ Have a pre-planned lesson or activity ready to use at a moment's notice. Many times assemblies are cancelled, guest speakers are unable to show up, or the copier breaks down just when you need it the most. Be prepared for these contingencies by having an activity ready to go.

✔ Make sure that students know how they are expected to behave outside of the classroom. Maintain the same standards outside the classroom as you do inside the classroom.

✔ Prepare students so that they know what to do when visitors enter the room. Teach them to expect interruptions so they will not be surprised when they occur.

✔ When an interruption occurs, keep the children productively occupied.

✔ Establish a procedure for students who arrive late. Students should know exactly where to go and what to do when entering late.

✔ Sharpening pencils should be a standardized practice. Students should know when they may not sharpen their pencils, how often, and how to go about doing it quietly.

✔ Tissue is almost a requirement in today's classroom. Students need to know where it is in the room, when they may use it, and how much they should take at one time.

✔ Using the bathroom and drinking fountain should not become abused procedures. Students need to know the appropriate times for using the bathroom or drinking fountain, whom they need to ask, and whether or not they need to sign out or obtain a hall pass.

Classroom Contingencies *(cont.)*

While you were gone . . .

Name_____ **Date** _____

The following is a list of assignments that your classmate, _____
_____ , gathered for you. Please complete as much of the
work as possible at home and bring it with you when you return. Make sure to
check in with your teacher(s) at an appropriate time your first day back. Get well
soon!

Subject	**Assignment**

Teacher Comments: _____

_____

_____

_____

_____

Checklist for Good Discipline

❏ Have your lessons clearly planned so students do not experience "down time."

❏ Keep parents informed about your class activities, discipline plan, homework, and how they can support your program.

❏ Set up simple, clear, class rules and teach them to the students.

❏ Have both consequences and rewards for appropriate behavior established with students.

❏ Communicate with parents early when a student is having problems at school.

❏ Follow school policy concerning suspensions, keeping students after school, and limiting recess or lunch time.

❏ Be consistent, fair, and positive with students.

❏ Plan how to reward students for completing work assignments.

❏ Help students to feel successful, and they will not need to use disruptions or negative behavior for attention.

❏ Plan for what students are to do if they have trouble completing their work or if they finish early.

❏ Consider alternating between quiet, individual activities and more energetic group activities.

How to. . . .

Keep Students Productive and Focused

Independent Work Time

Students work at various paces. Inevitably, when your students are working independently on an assignment, at least some of them will finish before the period is over. To prevent them from sitting idly and waiting for something else to do or distracting others who are still working, keep them productively occupied. The following ideas are just some of the ways you can do this. Choose a few and keep them posted so that your students know exactly what they may do if they finish early.

Things for Students to Do When They Finish Assignments Early

✔ Read a book from either the class or school library.

✔ Help other students. Research shows that helping others will significantly reinforce one's own learning.

✔ Write a letter. The celebrity addresses provided by *The Kid's Address Book* by Michael Levine makes writing to your favorite star easy.

✔ Draw a picture.

✔ Begin homework. This allows students with heavy after-school time commitments to lighten their loads and reduce their stress levels.

✔ Finish incomplete work.

✔ Study flash cards. Math facts and vocabulary words are just two of the many things that can be readily transferred to flash cards. Other flash card suggestions are provided on page 66.

✔ Use the class computer if you are lucky enough to have one.

✔ Play a quiet game. Concentration, a game which builds children's memories, is just one example. Games which can be used to supplement lessons or to productively engage small groups of students are provided on pages 60–64.

✔ Visit a learning center. See pages 67–70 for learning center activities.

✔ Help replace or redesign a class bulletin board.

✔ Clean and straighten desks, notebooks, portfolios, or classroom sets of books.

✔ Tend living class displays (terrarium, aquarium, indoor garden) by cleaning and adding food, water, etc.

Sponge Activities and Anytime Games

> *Frequently, teachers find themselves with an extra five or ten minutes here and there. We do not want to waste this time, yet we know there is not time to start a completely new activity. Sponge activities offer an excellent way to use these extra moments effectively. Sponge activities, which "soak up" the extra time, keep minds in "drive" instead of allowing students to shift them into neutral. The following is a list of some of the ways that you can use this extra time wisely.*

Sponge Activities for Transition Periods

A sponge activity may be given to students as they come into the room. Sponge activities can also serve to productively engage students in purposeful activities as teachers take care of necessary business like taking attendance, getting the lunch count, or collecting notes and homework. Sponge activities are also useful during transition periods while the teacher needs to reteach several students or to nudge someone into finishing. Sponge activities can be used to refocus students on something they have previously learned. For example, "Use your textbooks to find the names of three explorers that we talked about yesterday. Write their names and tell where they explored."

Or, the activities might be something like a puzzle, question, or problem to solve that is used to challenge students and keep them busy while the teacher takes care of his/her required paper work. You might challenge your class to a question a day, like "Why is the sky blue?" It gives students a chance to make suppositions about something they will (or may) study later.

Good sponge activities give students an opportunity to review, talk, or write about something they have learned. Sponges are best if they can be posted for the students to read when they are ready to complete the activity.

Anytime Games

A variety of games can be used as part of the sponge activities or to supplement regular lesson plans. In addition to the enjoyment students derive from these games, math, reading, and language skills are reinforced. Be sure to choose games that are appropriate for the grade level of the students. Model with the students first to be sure they understand all rules and directions.

Suggestions for sponge activities and anytime games can be found on pages 61–64.

60

Sponge Activities and Anytime Games *(cont.)*

Twenty Questions

Variations of this game are limited by the rule that all questions must be phrased in such a way as to be answered yes or no.

Safari

With a certain category in mind, such as fruits, the teacher says, "I'm going on a safari, and I'm taking a banana." The students try to guess the category and come up with another example. For instance, a student could say, "I'm going on a safari, and I'm bringing a bear." If the student's example falls under the teacher's category, the teacher invites the student to come along on the safari. If not, the teacher says, "I'm sorry, you cannot come." Keep playing until all understand the category.

Charades

The words or phrases to be guessed must be acted out in pantomime by members of teams.

Simon Says

You can also try "Opposite Simon Says" with your students. You say one thing, and your students do the exact opposite.

Hangman

Because of this word's connotations, many prefer to call it "Hang Spider." You may want to call it "Hang Pumpkin" in October, "Hang Turkey" in November, and then continue to change the name seasonally.

Around the World

The game begins when one student stands behind another. Ask a question, and the first student to answer it correctly moves behind the next student. The other sits down. Keep playing until you have moved around the entire classroom.

Thinking and Drinking

A wonderful way to review material, "Thinking and Drinking" begins when the teacher asks a question about some topic the class has been studying. When a student answers a question correctly, the teacher says, "You're thinking, so you're drinking." That student is then allowed to get a drink of water. Playing this game right after P.E. alleviates the crowding at the drinking fountain that often occurs when all the students drink at once.

The One-Two-Three Game

The students sit in a circle, and one at a time they tell the class how they are currently doing. "One" means very well, "three" means not very well, and "two" means somewhere in between. This is a great way to begin a day before proceeding with business as usual.

Sponge Activities and Anytime Games *(cont.)*

Up and Down Words

Students may work in pairs to complete the activity. They will need a dictionary, paper, and pencils. To play, they must choose a word and write it down the left side of the paper. Then, directly across from the letters write the same word up the right side of the paper (see diagram at right). To play, write a word on each line using the letter on the left as the first letter of the word and the letter on the right as the last letter of the word. The first player writes a word while the second player checks the correct spelling in the dictionary. Roles reverse back and forth for the rest of the game. A simple scoring system can be employed: Players receive five points for each correctly spelled word and one point for each letter in the word. If the students find this game is too difficult, allow both players to search together to find appropriate words in a dictionary.

Slider

This spelling and vocabulary game may be played by two individuals or two teams. To play the game, you will need to draw a grid on the chalkboard or overhead projector. (If two individuals play together they may use graph paper or a copy of page 64.) Start with a category such as sports, rivers, or farm animals. The first player on the first team goes to the chalkboard and writes a word in that category. If the word is correctly spelled, he scores one point for each letter in the word, but if the word is spelled incorrectly, the player loses a turn. Now the first player on the next team must build his word on the letters of the word already on the board. Play continues with teams taking turns writing words that connect with letters already on the board. Words may go across or down only, and they may not rest on top of or right next to another word. See the diagram at the left for a possible game configuration.

Tic-Tac-Toe Review

Draw a tic-tac-toe grid on the chalkboard or overhead projector. Divide the students into two teams. One team will represent X and the other team will represent O. Prepare drill cards in advance—sight words, basic math facts, contractions, etc. Show a card to the first person on the first team. If his response is correct, the player can place an X anywhere on the board for his team. An incorrect response results in a loss of a turn.

Now the other team must answer correctly in order to place an O on the board. Play continues with teams taking turns until one team is able to get three in a row. **Note:** Prepare 30–40 drill cards so that more than one game can be played. Some other skills that can be reviewed are abbreviations, states and their capitals, equivalent fractions, synonyms, antonyms, homonyms, spelling words, letter or number sequence, Roman numerals, colors, shapes, compound words, and plurals.

Sponge Activities and Anytime Games *(cont.)*

Alphabetical Sentences

Write a group of four or five letters on the chalkboard. Instruct the students to write sentences in which the words begin with the same letters in the same order as they appear on the chalkboard. For example, if the letters are STMP, students could write "Start the motor, please," or "Simba tasted mince pie." A variation of this idea is writing alliterative sentences. Direct students to write a sentence in which all (or most of) the words begin with the same sound as their first name. For example, Chris may write, "Crazy creepy crawlies climbed the cozy cavern." Share the sentences in small or large groups.

Simple Secret Codes

Display a code (see sample below) or make copies for each pair or group of students. Direct the students to write a short story or secret message using the code. Then have them exchange papers with other pairs or groups and decode the story or message.

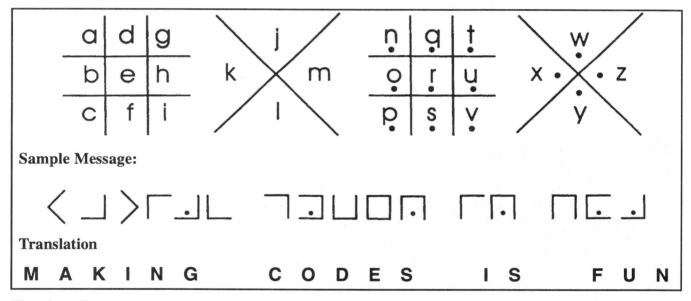

Five in a Row

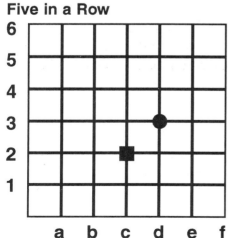

Draw a graph grid on the chalkboard or overhead projector. Label the horizontal axis with letters; label the vertical axis with numerals (see diagram at left). Divide the students into two teams. The first person on Team I (●)) calls out coordinates—e.g., c, 2. The first person on Team II (■)) must plot the coordinates with a square correctly on the grid, or he loses his turn. The next person on Team II calls out coordinates for the next person on Team I to plot a circle on the grid. Team members may not help one another. The object is for one team to get five coordinates in a row while the other team tries to block its efforts.

Sponge Activities and Anytime Games *(cont.)*

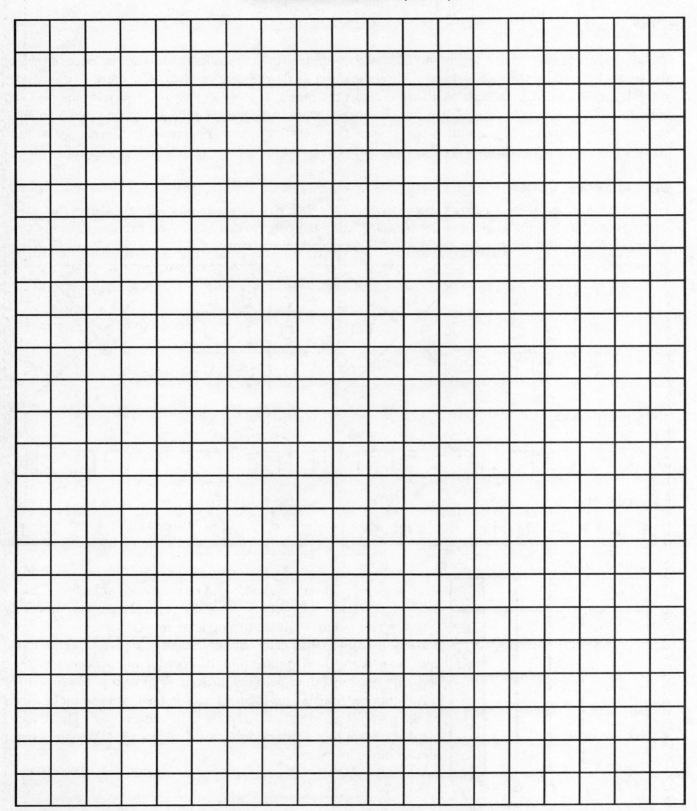

64

Prompts

Prompts are especially effective in the morning when the students first enter the room. Seeing one of the following prompts on the board reminds students that they are expected to get seated and get working quickly.

Name one thing we learned yesterday/today about . . .

Be ready to state three reasons for/characteristics of . . .

Come up with an example of . . .

Be ready to share a question you had about yesterday's lesson on . . .

Create a question that would be good to include on a test about . . .

Make up a sentence using this/these word(s) . . .

Describe/summarize in two sentences the . . .

Tell how you would solve this problem . . .

What do you think were the most important points made during . . .

Flash Cards

Flash cards offer a quick, simple way for students to learn new information. Excellent for a sponge activity, flash cards can be used individually, with partners, or with the entire class. There is almost no limit to the amount or variety of information that can be made into a set of flashcards. The following are just some of them.

Flash Card Ideas

Math facts—Place multiplication tables, addition, or subtraction problems on one side and answers on the back.

Spelling words—Done with partners, these cards have the spelling words on one side and nothing on the back. The two students take turns quizzing each other. These cards are excellent for building up the sight-word vocabulary of younger children.

Vocabulary words—Place words on one side, definitions on the other.

Geography cards—Place the shapes and drawings of the locations on one side, their names on the back.

States and capitals cards—Place the state names on one side and the capitals on the other.

Foreign language cards—Write a foreign word on one side, its English translation on the back.

Classification cards—Write categories on one side, examples of items in that category on the other.

Procedures—Write the name of a procedure on one side, the steps of the procedure on the back.

Total physical response cards—A word is written on one side of the card, and students respond to the word either by acting out its meaning or by pointing out an example of the word in the room. For example, a card could have "red" written on it, and the student would have to point to something in the room that is red.

Historical situation cards—On one side, a historical situation is named, such as the struggle for women's suffrage in the 1920's in the Northeast. On the back are listed the conditions and characteristics of that situation.

Mnemonic devices—Using an example from a previous list, one could write the word "HOMES" on one side and the names of the lakes Huron, Ontario, Michigan, Erie, and Superior on the other.

Learning Centers

Learning centers should be mind-stimulating places. As such, they become effective engines for skill development and practice, fostering creativity, and building responsibility and independence. They also allow students who have finished their assignments early to stay productively occupied. You may want to vary your centers throughout the year, offering different choices at different times. Also, it is a good idea to make centers available to more than one student at a time so that students have the opportunity to work with others. The following general center ideas will enable you to highlight and enrich various elements of your curriculum.

Setting Up Learning Centers

Centers are instructional work stations that are away from a student's regular work seat. The materials and activities set up in centers need to be designed so that students are able to complete them with little or no assistance from an adult. Some teachers use volunteers or older students to monitor and help students who are working at centers; other teachers use centers as a method for teaching responsibility and independence, as students are expected to complete most of the activities on their own. Centers can be set up on almost any subject and can be complete activities in themselves, or they can be an extension of something on which the class is working (i.e., science investigations where students have time to examine something "up close"). Centers can be structured and detailed, very creative, or even as simple as setting up jigsaw puzzles. Use your imagination and creativity to set up centers that will be exciting, challenging, and interesting to students.

Some teachers ask if centers have a place in a whole language classroom. Students still need opportunities to work individually, to be responsible for completing assignments on their own, and to have an opportunity to make choices about what they do. All of this can be accomplished by working at centers in the classroom.

Things to Keep in Mind When Setting Up Centers

1. Have some form of symbolic directions for students (or anyone who might be helping students) even if you orally explain the center. These symbols are for students who are not yet reading.

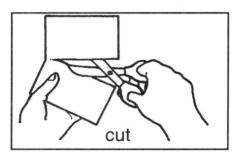

cut

paste

write

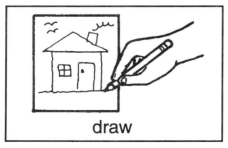

draw

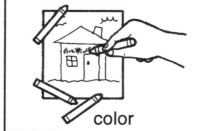

color

read

Learning Centers *(cont.)*

Setting Up Learning Centers *(cont.)*

2. Decorate centers so that they are inviting to students. Have a partially completed model for students to see so that they know what they are expected to do. Use the bottom part of a bulletin board, a chart taped to a wall, a wooden stand, or a cardboard display to post directions and models of completed work.

3. Have all materials that students will need at the center so that students will not have to interrupt to get glue, scissors, etc. Folders or boxes are useful so that students remember where to put the center supplies when they are finished or when time is up.

Name:		
	Color, Cut, Paste	
	Red Apple	
	Yellow Banana	
	Brown Bread	
	Blue Ball	

4. Have a plan for students to record which centers they have completed. Here is a sample recording sheet. A blank regular-sized copy is included on page 71.

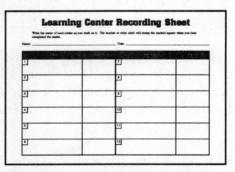

Learning Center Recording Sheet

5. Design a method for students to check their own work at centers whenever possible. Perhaps a parent could help check for accuracy of work if you set the standards. The record sheet discussed above has a place for an assistant or the teacher to check that the work was completed. The column could be used to indicate accuracy or correctness of the assignment when it is checked by either the student or an adult. This might be done on a weekly or monthly basis.

6. Centers can be used for two different purposes. Students work at centers whenever they finish their regular assignments. They also work at centers at an assigned time during the week when the teacher works with smaller groups of children on enrichment assignments or reteaching concepts that were missed earlier. By setting up enough activities for a week or month, the teacher is free from continually thinking about setting up more centers. The best centers are often those that follow some class instruction, but all centers need not relate to a specific area of study. On the following page is a partial list of centers.

Learning Center Suggestions

Science Center—Use this for experiments, observations, reading, worksheets, use of equipment such as microscopes, hand lenses, etc.

Game Center—Stock this with purchased games, teacher- or student-made games, electronic games, puzzles, word searches, crossword puzzles, and others. You may wish to send students to the Game Center as a reward for exemplary conduct. See pages 60–64 for the game suggestions.

Art Center—This is helpful for special projects, holiday or monthly theme ideas, experimentation with different media (clay, water colors, toothpicks, etc.), or a project linked to the current curriculum. Put out whatever art supplies are available and let your students dazzle you with their creativity.

Writing Center—This is designed for work on journals, reports, prompt-generated or free writing, vocabulary charts with words from some area being studied, and student-made little books for other students to read.

Reading Center—Stock this with magazines, poetry, books, newspaper articles, or other material displayed for students to read on specific topics, a unit being studied, or selections by a particular author.

Skill Center—This should have plenty of flash cards, simulations, or other drill activities on particular skills.

Listening Center—Supply with cassettes, records, recorders, and/or radios displayed for students to listen and respond to by drawing, writing, worksheets, etc.

Research Center—Along with dictionary, thesaurus, encyclopedia, atlas, etc., supply with specific research activities from task cards or worksheets.

Post Office Center—This is a writing center where students write postcards, notes, or letters to each other and then deliver them to mailboxes set up for each student, the teacher, principal, and others as needed. (Teachers use empty ice cream containers, cardboard shoe storage boxes, or wooden "cubbies" for mail boxes.) In addition, Michael Levine's *The Kids' Address Book* allows students to correspond with their favorite stars.

Library Center—Provide a collection of 200–300 books, both fiction and nonfiction, that students can choose to read alone or with a partner. Activities can be designed as follow-up to reading of these books. Written book reports, mobiles, dioramas, oral projects, and book jacket designs are but a few of the things that can be rotated at the library center as follow-up activities. Arrangements can be made for students to borrow books from the library center by setting up a simple filing system. An index card with the book title and a place for the student's signature can be placed in each book. When students check out books, they simply sign their names on the index cards and place them in a file box located at the library center.

Learning Center Suggestions *(cont.)*

Puppet Center—This becomes a creative center where students can plan a story to use with commercial or student-created puppets. Students can work with partners or small groups on their "show." Perhaps once a week, time can be set aside for the presentations that are ready. Puppets that can be designed by students include stick (tongue depressor or ice cream sticks), paper bag, sock, finger and felt.

Puppet stages can be included in the puppet center. The type of puppet stages include the following:

✔ **Table:** Hang an old sheet over a low table. The puppeteers simply kneel on the floor behind the table. The puppets move on top of the table.

✔ **Box:** Cut a large square hole in the top half of a big box. Prop up the box securely. The puppeteers sit or kneel behind the box. The puppets move in the square hole.

✔ **Sheet:** Hang a rope or heavy string across a corner of the room about 2 feet (60 cm) from the floor. Drop a sheet over the rope. The puppeteers kneel behind the sheet in the corner. The puppets move above the sheet.

Listening Center—Students follow along in their books as they listen to stories on tape.

Dramatic Arts Center—Equipped with hats, masks, costumes, and props, this center allows students to explore the world of drama.

Math Center—Students can practice sorting, grouping, sequencing or other math skills by using manipulatives. You can increase the effectiveness of math centers by relating the activities to the literature selections your class is studying at the time.

Concentration Center—This center strengthens students' memories with practice activities and challenges.

Make and Break Center—Using magnetic letters and a magnetic board, choose a word such as "Book" with a common stem (-ook) and an initial letter (b). Have the students replace the initial letter and form as many words as they can and record them. This is a great way to improve the reading and spelling skills of primary grade students.

Sentence Strips Center—Given the words of a sentence, each on a separate strip, the student's goal is to place the words in the proper order, copy the sentence onto a piece of paper, and illustrate it.

70

Learning Center Recording Sheet

Write the name of each center as you work on it. The teacher or other adult will stamp the marked square when you have completed the center.

Name: _____

Date: _____

	Center	Completed		Center	Completed
1			7		
2			8		
3			9		
4			10		
5			11		
6			12		

Learning Center Signs

To help identify your centers, reproduce the signs on the following pages, color them, and hang each at the appropriate center. You might choose to reproduce them onto index paper and color them with crayons or colored pencils. Laminate them for durability.

They may be used at the centers in a variety of ways.

✔ Tape them to the wall.

✔ Punch two holes on either side of the sign and run yarn or wire through the holes. Hang the yarn over a nail or hook.

✔ Punch a hole and put it over a nail.

✔ Make a clothespin stand. Cut a tennis ball in half with a craft knife or scissors. Line both halves with plastic wrap. Fill halves with plaster of Paris. Place one paper towel roll tube into each ball, pressing gently so that the tube remains straight; allow plaster to dry thoroughly. Peel away tennis ball and plastic wrap. Paint plaster, tube and the two clothespins with tempera paint; allow to dry. Attach one clothespin holding the sign to the top of each paper towel tube. Display at the center.

Learning Center Signs (cont.)

This Center Is Closed

This Center Is Open

Learning Center Signs *(cont.)*

Writing Center

Social Studies Center

Learning Center Signs *(cont.)*

Drama and Stories Center

Art Center

Learning Center Signs *(cont.)*

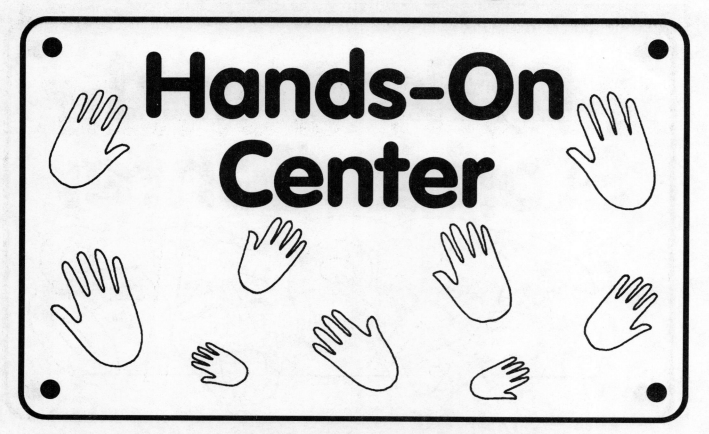

Hands-On Center

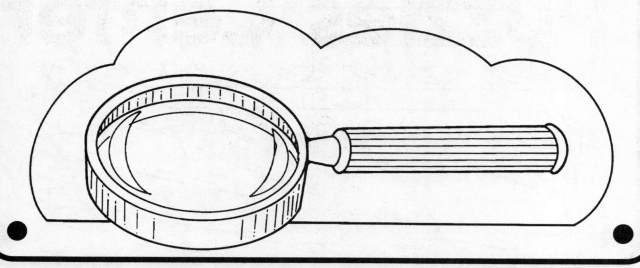

Science Center

Learning Center Signs (cont.)

Math Center

Games and Puzzles Center

And Last...

but

Not Least

How to Reduce First Day Jitters

The first day of school can be a very traumatic experience for elementary school children, not to mention elementary school teachers! The following activities have been compiled in order to help alleviate some of the understandable nervousness. Use some or all of them to ease your way into a successful year.

Suggestions for Easing into the First Day of School

✔ Model enthusiasm. Students are more likely to be excited if they see their teacher being excited.

✔ Contact your students before the year begins to introduce yourself. This may not be possible at your school. If it is, you can either do it over the telephone or by postcard.

✔ Memorize, if possible, the names of your students before the school year begins. Obtain a copy of the previous yearbook or class picture and study the names and pictures. Hope that nobody gets a haircut over the summer!

✔ Have name tags waiting for the students as they walk in the door. Use one yourself.

✔ Take your class on a tour of the school. This relieves student anxiety that comes from not knowing the location of such places as the office, cafeteria, or restroom.

✔ Give the class some seatwork to complete and call each student up to see you, one at a time. Ask each one if it is all right for you to send a note home telling the parent(s) what a nice job that student has done that day. To say that your students will be pleasantly surprised is a vast understatement.

✔ Sit the students in a circle and try the following activities:

Pairing off—Have students pair off with others they do not know. After they have spoken with each other for a few minutes, reassemble the circle and have all the students introduce their partners to the rest of the group. For younger students, it may be helpful to provide questions for them to ask one another.

Name Game—Have students introduce themselves to the class, starting with an adjective which begins with the same letter as their name. Examples include Happy Helen. Students are much more likely to remember names when they are presented in this way.

Rearrange the circle—Have the students stand and move to the center of the circle. Then ask them to sit back down in the order of their birthdays or alphabetically. This activity builds communication skills, and it also allows you to determine who some potential leaders in your class may be.

People Hunt—Distribute a People Hunt sheet containing various descriptions or characteristics of people. Have students mingle until they find others who match these descriptions and get their sheets signed by these people. Please see the sample People Hunt sheets on the following pages.

Toss the Ball—Divide your class into groups of about eight and give each group a ball. Within each group, have the students form a circle and take turns throwing the ball to everyone in the group. The thrower must say the name of the student to whom he or she is throwing. After catching the ball, the receiver must use the proper name to thank the thrower for throwing the ball to him/her. This is a great way to learn names.

People Hunt

Find a person who . . .　　　　　　　　　**Name**

1.　. . . can name four science fiction books.　　_____

2.　. . . has the same favorite food as I do.　　_____

3.　. . . has a birthday in December.　　_____

4.　. . . is interested in_____.　　_____
　　　　　　　　　(Name a hobby.)

5.　. . . likes to bake.　　_____

6.　. . . can spell_____
　　　　　　　(Add a word.)
　　　without looking at this paper.　　_____

7.　. . . has the same color hair that I have.　　_____

8.　. . . has a brother or sister at this school.　　_____

9.　. . . knows what "fragile" means.　　_____

10.　. . . knows the three steps to any
　　　column problem.　　_____

People Hunt

Find . . .   **Name**

1. A person who has more than four
   brothers and sisters.   _____

2. Someone born in the same month I was.   _____

3. A student who speaks two languages.   _____

4. Somebody taller than I am.   _____

5. Someone born in a different state.   _____

6. Someone I did not know last year.   _____

7. A student who plays Little League.   _____

8. A person who has *The Cat in the Hat*
   at home.   _____

9. Someone who can name three presidents.   _____

10. A student who has the same favorite
    ice cream as I do.   _____

People Hunt

Find a person . . .   **Name**

1. Who can name five Dr. Seuss books.   _____

2. Who has the same favorite color as I do.   _____

3. Who has a birthday during the summer.   _____

4. Who went to kindergarten at _____.   _____

5. Who likes broccoli.   _____

6. Who can spell *Mississippi* without looking
   at the ceiling or at this paper.   _____

7. Who has the same color eyes that I have.   _____

8. Who has an older brother and an older sister.   _____

9. Who knows what *transparent* means.   _____

10. Who knows what month comes after June.   _____

People Search

Name _____

Directions: Find people in the class who fit the following descriptions and have them initial the appropriate box.

Find someone who . . .

. . . has lived in a different state. Which one?

_____

. . . plays a musical instrument. Which instrument?

_____

. . . stays up late at night. What time?

_____

. . . collects something. What is it?

_____

. . . loves vegetables. Name a favorite.

_____

. . . owns an unusual pet. What is it?

_____

. . . has read a good book lately. What is it?

_____

. . . plays a sport after school. What is it?

Back-to-School Night

Back-to-School Night can be a fine opportunity to meet with the parents of your students. At the same time, it can be nerve-wracking to plan and coordinate. Here are a few suggestions and ideas that will help make the evening pleasant and successful.

Since this may be the first time you meet many of the parents, it may be helpful to view the event as the parent's first day of school. With this thought in mind, you may want to consult the How-to-Reduce-First-Day-Jitters list on page 79 and employ some of the same ideas that you used with your students on their first day of school.

Back-to- School Night Suggestions

✔ Ask your students to deliver personalized invitations to their parents that they themselves made. Try to have these invitations delivered about a week prior to the event.

✔ The day after the students deliver these invitations, begin a daily "Countdown to Back-to-School Night." Have your students deliver one strip per day until the day of the event. Please see the insert on page 85 for a sample countdown sheet. The sheet you will find was used to promote one classroom's annual Community Festival.

✔ Have the parents sign in as they enter the classroom.

✔ Have student-created name tags waiting for the parents as they enter the room.

✔ Place the name tags on the students' individual desks so the parents can sit in the same seats as their children.

✔ Try to simulate an actual school day as much as possible so that parents can appreciate what it feels like to be a student in your class. For example, if music is playing in your class each morning as the students arrive, play music as the parents arrive.

✔ Start off the evening with some of the ice-breaking activities in which the students participated on the first day of school in order to build comradery among the parents.

✔ Introduce yourself and the aide, if possible, and briefly discuss some or all of the following: the major aspects of the curriculum, the goals/mission statement of your class, your homework policy, the classroom management system, the home-school communication system, and any issue of special interest or importance to you.

✔ Allow time for the parents to ask questions.

✔ Be careful about offering specific information about individual students to any parents. With so many people around, there really is not time for one-on-one conversations. If parents ask you about their child, try to arrange a meeting for some time in the near future.

✔ The next day, call or send a note home thanking the parents for attending.

Sample Count Down

Only 7 days until the Community Festival!

Tuesday, April 25th at 7:30 in Room 8. Hope to see you there.

Only 6 days until the Community Festival!

Tuesday, April 25th at 7:30 in Room 8. Bring your camera.

Only 5 days until the Community Festival!

Tuesday, April 25th at 7:30 in Room 8. The event of the year!

Only 4 days until the Community Festival!

Tuesday, April 25th at 7:30 in Room 8. Fun for the whole family!

Only 1 day until the Community Festival!

Tuesday, April 25th at 7:30 in Room 8. See you tomorrow!

Parent Conferences

> *Planning ahead can greatly reduce the stress and hassle of parent conference time. It is never too early to start preparing. Start documenting student behavior and performance on day one. If you have built and maintained a solid line of communication with parents from the outset, then conference time should not be a time for surprise or frustration. This list will help you with the preparation process.*

Parent Conferencing Tips

Setting Up the Conference

✔ Send home a list of dates and times that you are available for conferencing, from which the parents can choose three.

✔ Upon return of this sheet, select one and alert the parents as to which time you have chosen as well as to the procedure for rescheduling or cancelling. Just as with your students, be very clear with the parents as to what you would like them to do. Please see the insert on page 88 for a sample conference confirmation form.

✔ Request that the child be present during the conference. It will be one of the few times all year when you can give each child your total attention for an extended period of time.

Preparing for the Conference

✔ Review the student's cumulative record.

✔ Review your sheet documenting student behavior.

✔ Talk to other adults who come into contact with the student.

✔ Make a list of strengths and a list of areas in which the student needs to improve. Include no more than three on the latter. Index cards are effective for this purpose. You can fit each student's information on one card and then connect these index cards by punching a hole through each one and running a ring through them.

✔ Gather student work samples which illustrate the points you noted on the index cards.

✔ Rehearse what you are going to say during the conference.

Parent Conferences *(cont.)*

The Day of the Conference

✔ Provide a private, comfortable setting. Place some chairs outside the room in case the next parents arrive early.

✔ Welcome the parent. Smile and make eye contact.

✔ Avoid sitting across the table from parents. Doing so gives the meeting an adversarial tone; sitting next to parents sets a friendlier tone.

✔ Express appreciation for the parents' coming and establish a rapport by talking informally for a few moments at the outset.

✔ Begin the conference on a positive note. Share a specific example of the child's exemplary work or behavior.

✔ Continue discussing the child's strengths. Be specific and have evidence to support your statements.

✔ Discuss no more than three areas in which the child needs improvement.

✔ Discuss ways in which the parents can help bring about this improvement.

✔ Ask the parents for their questions, comments, or suggestions.

✔ Check to make sure that everything you discussed is clear to them.

✔ Remind the parents of the procedure for reaching you at school.

✔ End on a positive note and thank the parents again for coming.

Conference Follow-Up

✔ Send a note home thanking the parents for attending the conference.

✔ Call parents the first time the child shows improvement in one of the areas you highlighted.

✔ Remind them that your door is always open.

Conference Form

Dear Parents,

Our Conference is scheduled for _____, _____

at _____ in Room _____.

I am looking forward to meeting with you to discuss your child's progress.

Please come prepared with any questions of your own; you may list them on the response sheet below.

Return the bottom section of this form to me by _____.

day and date

I am looking forward to meeting you.

Yours truly,

_____
Homeroom Teacher

Student's Name: _____

Teacher: _____ Room: _____

Scheduled Conference Date: _____

Time: _____

☐ Yes, I am able to meet you at our scheduled time.

☐ No, I will be unable to meet you at the scheduled time. Please call me to determine another time that is convenient for us both.

I would like to discuss the following:_____

_____

_____

_____
Parent Name (Please Print)

Plans for the Substitute

Whenever you are absent for the day, it is important for your students' well-being that you leave your substitute all the information he/she will need to have a productive day. Your diligent preparation will result in a smoother-running day, an appreciative substitute, and grateful students.

Things to Let a Substitute Know

✔ Class rules, rewards, and consequences

✔ Your signal for getting the student's attention

✔ Names of three or four reliable students (including one designated special helper)

✔ Class schedule

✔ The homework due and the homework to be assigned

✔ Location of major supplies, lunch cards, and playground equipment

✔ School map

✔ The name of a teacher to whom the substitute can turn for help

✔ The hours and duties of the aide

✔ A special game the class enjoys playing

✔ Any team-teaching arrangement which you have with other teachers

✔ Any special needs some of your students may have, such as taking medication

✔ Pre-planned lessons which can be delivered with ease

✔ A reminder to let the students know that you are all right. (This is important because students do worry about you.)

Emergency Substitute Plans

Create an emergency substitute folder by duplicating pages 90–93 and filling them out as completely as possible. (Note: Add pages with generic subject area assignments, as well as a literature selection to be read to the class, directions for some favorite physical education games, a class list, a map of the school, and special directions for rainy days, assemblies, or contingency plans for minimum days.) When these pages are completed, glue them to the front and back of a manila folder. This folder should be kept up to date as any information or directions change.

Regular Substitute Plans

When you know ahead of time that you will be away from your class, you need to leave plans that are more detailed than you probably write for yourself. Some of the notes and page numbers that might be enough for you will need to be clarified for a substitute. Preparing a step-by-step plan for the day may take extra time, but it will be worth it if you do not have to reteach what should have been taught while you were away.

Leave the emergency substitute folder whenever you are going to be absent, but caution the substitute to use your regular plans if at all possible. There is a lot of information in the substitute folder that will be helpful in either case.

Substitute Folder

Teacher: _____ **Assistant:** _____

Regular Time Schedule (including library, computer lab, music, etc., and different locations where applicable)

TIME	MONDAY	TUESDAY	WEDNESDAY	THURSDAY	FRIDAY

Helpful students: _____

_____

Teacher(s) to call for assistance: _____

_____

Children with special needs or health problems: _____

_____

Plans for the Substitute

People at our school you might need to know:

- Principal: _____

- Secretary: _____

- Nurse: _____

- Custodian: _____

How to get . . .

- Art Supplies: _____

- Audio/Visual Equipment: _____

- Custodial Help: _____

- Teacher Lunch: _____

Emergency Signals and Drills:

- Fire Drill _____

    Sounds like: _____

    What to do: _____

- Earthquake Drill

    Sounds like: _____

    What to do: _____

- Other: _____

Discipline and Classroom Management

- Quiet Signal: _____

- Discipline Program: _____

  _____

  _____

- Rewards: _____

  _____

  _____

Classroom Rules: _____

_____

_____

_____

_____

_____

Classroom Routines:

- Pencil Sharpener: _____

- Drinks: _____

- Restroom: _____

- Illness: _____

- Office: _____

Discipline and Classroom Management *(cont.)*

Positive rewards or awards we use include these: _____

_____

_____

Teacher's manuals are located . . . _____

_____

Regular lesson plans are located . . . _____

_____

_____

Duty schedule is located . . . _____

_____

_____

Special Instructions: _____

_____

_____

_____

_____

Please leave a note telling something that went well today as well as making me aware of problems. I like to be able to discuss how the the day went with the students as it teaches them responsibility. Please keep all parent notes and indicate who was absent. If there were students who were especially helpful, please let me know. I want to be able to reward them. Thank you for standing in for me today.

Classroom Assistants and Volunteers

Having a classroom assistant or volunteer is becoming more and more necessary in the modern classroom. An assistant can greatly reduce your workload, serve as a sounding board off which you can bounce ideas, and offer valuable support to your students. In order to keep aides happy and enthusiastic about their work, attempt to integrate them as thoroughly as possible into your classroom routines. Generally, assistants are keenly aware of what goes on in the classroom. Sometimes they notice things the teacher does not. For this reason, seek out the opinion of your aide, for example, when it comes time, to write a test or when two students are having problems getting along. You may be surprised by the insights the aide brings to your attention. Your class will be that much stronger when the contributions of your assistant are solicited and valued.

The following list contains several ways your assistant can contribute to your classroom. If you decide to have your assistant work with individuals or small groups, avoid having him/her work only with students who are falling behind and are in need of extra help. Such a practice stigmatizes working with the aide and can embarrass the very students you are trying so hard to help.

Ways to Involve Classroom Assistants and Volunteers

✔ Checking off and recording homework and/or classwork

✔ Taking attendance—either verbally or visually

✔ Reading the children a story

✔ Putting up or changing the class bulletin boards

✔ Taking the students out to recess or lunch

✔ Individual tutoring

✔ Beginning a phone tree—calling the first parent on the list when a message needs to be relayed

✔ Getting supplies together for upcoming class projects

✔ Duplicating materials

✔ Working with a group of students

✔ Helping to prepare for parent conferences

✔ Helping to prepare tests

✔ Helping to establish a seating chart

✔ Monitoring a behavior or performance contract

✔ Recording the day's homework hotline

✔ Planning for class social events

✔ Circulating and supervising while students work independently

✔ Assembling the work packets for absent students (Please see the list on page 55, entitled "Planning for Contingencies" for more information about these work packets.)

✔ Putting up the Student-of-the-Week display

The School Environment

Often students see themselves solely as individuals or solely as members of one classroom. It is up to us as teachers to help students understand that they are part of a larger community called a school. Connections need to be made among teachers, among students, and between teachers and students. Here are some ideas which will help facilitate the process of making your school a better place for all.

How to Create a Better School Environment

✔ Plan cross-grade activities. For example, have kindergarteners dictate their own stories to fifth-graders who will then write them down. Then, together they can illustrate the stories.

✔ Arrange for classes of similar ages to work together on special projects. Neighborhood clean-ups are one such possibility.

✔ Invite other classes to attend special performances by your class.

✔ Emphasize to your students the importance of walking quietly in the hallways while other classes are at work.

✔ Ask your students to pick up any trash they may see during the day. This applies both inside and outside the classroom.

✔ On the playground teach your students not to run through other classes' physical education or recess activities.

✔ Compliment other teachers and students when you notice or have heard about something positive or creative they have done.

✔ Encourage your students to write letters of praise to any staff member or student whom they notice performing well. This idea works very well as part of a letter-writing center.

✔ Initiate a "Reading Buddy" Program with another classroom. In a Reading Buddy Program, a class of upper-grade students works one-on-one with a class of primary students to improve the latter's reading skills. The older children experience the feeling of being needed and appreciated while the younger students benefit from the assistance and undivided attention of older friends. Feel free to expand this activity to include activities other than reading. This kind of cross-age tutoring also results in learning gains for the older children. Information about the Reading Buddy program is provided on page 32.

✔ Hang a large poster in your room on which any member of your class community can record the accomplishments or good deeds of others. Your classroom community will be strengthened when its citizens have the opportunity to recognize publicly the exemplary actions of other community members.

Sample Reading Buddy Program Letter

October 20, 199_____

Loyola Village School
22 Whale Lane
Cedar Point, Oregon

Dear Student,

    Starting soon, you will have the opportunity to serve as a reading buddy for the students of Room 20. As a reading buddy, you will work one-on-one with a student from Room 20 to help improve his/her reading skills. If you are worried that you do not know how to help someone with his or her reading, please don't be. After some short training sessions, you will be ready to get started. Once you see how much you are helping these kids, you will feel very proud of yourself. It will also be fun. If you are interested in being a reading buddy, sign your name at the bottom of this page, tear it off, and return it to me as soon as possible. The first training session will be next week.

        Sincerely,

        Mr. Reifman

- -

Yes, I am interested in being a reading buddy.

Name _____